The Beginner's Blueprint to Day Trading Futures

Master Oil, Gold & Index Futures with Simple, Proven Strategies

By Grant Westbrook

First Edition

Table of Contents

Introduction: Why Trade Futures?

If you've ever dreamed of making money from the markets—but felt overwhelmed by complicated charts, conflicting advice, or information overload—you're in the right place. This book is your beginner-friendly blueprint to day trading one of the most powerful and exciting markets in the world: **futures.**

Futures markets offer a unique edge to retail traders. They're **highly liquid**, **cost-efficient**, and **accessible 24 hours a day**, making them ideal for people who want to trade part-time, full-time, or even just before or after work. Whether you're interested in crude oil, gold, or stock market indices like the S&P 500 and Nasdaq, these markets provide **scalable opportunities** with relatively low capital compared to traditional stocks.

Unlike buying and holding long-term investments, day trading futures lets you take advantage of **short-term price movements**—whether the market is going up or down. This gives you the flexibility to profit in **any market condition**, using a focused, rule-based approach.

But let's be honest—futures trading isn't a get-rich-quick scheme. It takes **discipline, strategy, and structure**. That's exactly what this book delivers.

You won't find vague theories or overloaded technical jargon here. Instead, you'll get:

- **Step-by-step explanations** of how futures contracts work
- **Clear, beginner-friendly breakdowns** of oil, gold, and index futures
- **Simple trading setups** that anyone can follow
- **Essential risk management** techniques to protect your capital
- And most importantly—**a repeatable game plan** to go from curious beginner to confident trader

Throughout this book, you'll learn how to trade smart—not impulsively—by focusing on what actually works. You'll discover how professional traders think, how they manage risk, and how you can apply the same logic to your own strategy, even if you're starting with a small account.

No experience? No problem. By the end of this book, you'll have a full understanding of how futures markets work and exactly what to do each day when you sit down to trade.

Let’s get started. Your journey to becoming a profitable futures trader begins now

Chapter 1

Futures Trading 101 – What You Need to Know First

Introduction

Before diving into strategies, charts, or trade setups, you need a rock-solid understanding of what futures are, how they work, and why they offer such an incredible opportunity for day traders. This chapter lays the groundwork and clears up common misconceptions so you can start trading with clarity and confidence.

What Are Futures?

Futures are standardized financial contracts that obligate the buyer to purchase (or the seller to sell) a specific asset at a predetermined price on a set future date. But here's the key: as a **day trader**, you're not holding until expiration. You're trading the **price movement** of these contracts intraday—just like you would with stocks.

Example: A crude oil futures contract might represent 1,000 barrels of oil. But as a trader, you're not taking delivery of oil—you're just trading price moves, in and out, for potential profit.

Why Trade Futures Over Stocks or Forex?

Futures markets offer several advantages:

- **High Leverage**: You can control large positions with relatively small capital.
- **24-Hour Access**: Trade nearly around the clock, five days a week.
- **Low Fees & No Pattern Day Trader Rule**: Great for small accounts.
- **Highly Liquid**: Major contracts like oil and the S&P 500 futures have tight spreads.
- **Volatility**: Perfect for short-term traders seeking quick price action.

What Assets Can You Trade?

The futures market covers a wide range of asset classes:

1. **Crude Oil (CL)** – High volatility, excellent for scalping and momentum trades.

2. **Gold (GC)** – Safe-haven asset with smooth technical behavior.

3. **E-mini S&P 500 (ES)** – Tracks the top 500 U.S. companies, heavily traded.

4. **E-mini Nasdaq (NQ)** – High-growth tech exposure, very fast-moving.

5. **Mini Dow (YM)** – Represents the Dow Jones 30, a bit slower than ES/NQ.

For beginners, focusing on **just 1 or 2 markets** helps develop consistency and rhythm.

Key Futures Terms You Must Know

Contract: The standardized agreement to buy or sell a specific quantity of an asset.

Tick Size: The smallest price movement. Each market has its own tick value (e.g., ES = $12.50 per tick).

Margin: The amount of capital required to open a position.

Leverage: Your ability to control more with less. Can magnify profits—and losses.

Expiration Date: Futures contracts expire, but day traders rarely hold that long.

Volume & Open Interest: Measures of market activity and liquidity.

Who Are You Trading Against?

The futures market is a **zero-sum game**—for every winner, there's a loser. You'll be trading against:

- Retail traders (like yourself)
- Hedge funds
- Banks
- Algorithms and institutional traders

Success comes from understanding how these players behave and learning to trade **with** the momentum, not against it.

Do You Need a Lot of Money to Start?

No. Thanks to **micro futures contracts** like **Micro E-mini S&P (MES)** and **Micro Nasdaq (MNQ)**, you can start trading with as little as a few hundred dollars. These contracts offer:

- Smaller tick sizes
- Less risk per trade
- Ideal learning ground before moving to full-size contracts

Summary

Futures trading isn't as complex as it first appears. Once you understand the structure and advantages, it becomes clear why so many traders make futures their weapon of choice. You now know what futures are, how they differ from other markets, and why they're a prime tool for day trading.

Key Takeaways

✔ Futures are standardized contracts that allow you to profit from price movements without owning the asset.

✔ They offer high leverage, liquidity, and accessibility for traders of all experience levels.

✔ Focus on liquid markets like crude oil, gold, and index futures for consistent trade setups.

✔ Micro futures make it possible to start small and scale up as you gain skill.

✔ Knowing the basics gives you a strong foundation to build your trading strategy on.

Chapter 2

Understanding the Futures Markets – Key Concepts Every Beginner Must Know

Introduction

To succeed as a futures trader, you must first understand the foundational mechanics of how these markets work. Futures trading offers immense profit potential—but only for those who know the rules of the game. In this chapter, you'll learn the essential building blocks: what futures are, how they're traded, and the key market terminology every trader needs to master.

What Are Futures Contracts?

Futures contracts are standardized legal agreements to buy or sell a specific asset at a predetermined price on a specific future date. Unlike spot trading (where assets are exchanged immediately), futures contracts are based on a promise for later delivery—but in practice, most traders never actually take delivery of the asset.

Key Features of Futures Contracts

Standardized: Each contract has a fixed quantity, expiration date, and tick value.

Traded on Exchanges: Futures are traded on centralized exchanges like CME (Chicago Mercantile Exchange), which ensures transparency and liquidity.

Leverage: Futures allow traders to control large positions with relatively small amounts of capital (margin).

Settlement Types: Some contracts are settled in cash (e.g., index futures), while others involve physical delivery (e.g., oil or grain).

Margin, Leverage & Maintenance

Understanding leverage and margin is critical in futures trading.

Margin:

- This is not a fee, but a **good-faith deposit** required to open a position.
- **Initial Margin** is what you need to enter a trade.
- **Maintenance Margin** is the minimum balance you must maintain to keep the position open.

Leverage:

- Futures naturally offer **high leverage**. For example, trading a crude oil contract may only require ~$5,000 margin to control over $80,000 worth of oil.
- **High leverage magnifies both gains and losses**—this is a double-edged sword.

Futures Symbols and Contract Specs

Each futures product has a unique symbol and specification. Learning to read these is part of your daily trader routine.

Example: Crude Oil (CL)

- **Ticker Symbol:** CL
- **Contract Size:** 1,000 barrels
- **Tick Size:** $0.01 per barrel = $10 per tick
- **Expiration:** Monthly

Example: S&P 500 E-mini (ES)

- **Ticker Symbol:** ES
- **Contract Size:** $50 x S&P 500 Index
- **Tick Size:** 0.25 = $12.50 per tick
- **Expiration:** Quarterly

Who Trades Futures?

There are two main participants in the futures markets:

- **Hedgers:** Use futures to protect against price fluctuations (e.g., farmers, airlines, oil producers).

- **Speculators:** Aim to profit from price movement without intention of delivery. This includes retail traders like you.

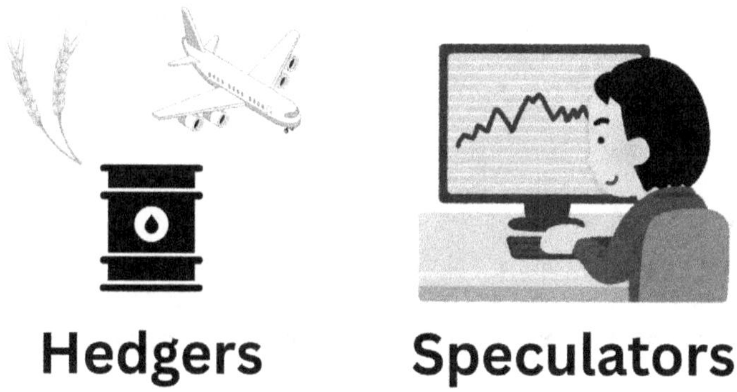

Futures vs. Stocks: Key Differences

Feature	Futures	Stocks
Ownership	No ownership (just a contract)	Equity in a company
Leverage	Built-in, much higher	Limited (via margin)
Trading Hours	Nearly 24 hours	Typically 9:30 AM – 4 PM ET
Short Selling	Easy, with no restrictions	Limited, often harder
Market Structure	Centralized exchanges	Varies across brokers

Types of Futures You'll Trade

We will focus on:

- **Crude Oil Futures (CL)**
- **Gold Futures (GC)**
- **Index Futures (ES, NQ)**

Each offers unique volatility, liquidity, and opportunity

Summary

Understanding the structure of the futures market gives you an edge. From margin and leverage to contract specs and trading hours, knowing these basics ensures you won't be caught off guard.

Key Takeaways

✔ Futures are standardized contracts traded on exchanges like CME.

✔ Leverage and margin let you control large positions with less capital, but increase risk.

✔ Most traders are speculators aiming to profit from price movements—not to take delivery.

✔ Learning contract specs and symbols is essential for quick and accurate trade execution.

✔ Futures differ from stocks in ownership, leverage, and trading hours.

Chapter 3

Setting Up Your Trading Platform – Tools, Charts, and Broker Selection

Introduction

Before you can execute your first trade, you need the right setup. This includes choosing a reliable broker, learning how to use your trading platform, and customizing your charts to support your trading style. In this chapter, we'll walk through the essential components of a professional trading environment so you can trade futures confidently and efficiently.

Choosing a Futures Broker

Your broker acts as the gateway to the futures markets, so it's important to choose one that fits your needs.

What to Look For in a Broker:

- **Low Commissions & Fees:** Trading costs can eat into your profits, so prioritize brokers with competitive pricing.
- **Platform Stability:** Look for brokers with reliable trading platforms that won't crash during high-volume times.
- **Margin Requirements:** Compare the initial and maintenance margin requirements.
- **Access to Futures Products:** Ensure the broker offers the contracts you plan to trade (e.g., CL, ES, GC).

- **Customer Support:** Quick, responsive support is critical—especially during fast market conditions.

Popular Futures Brokers:

- NinjaTrader
- TradeStation
- Interactive Brokers
- TD Ameritrade (via thinkorswim)

Setting Up Your Trading Platform

Most brokers offer their own platforms or integrate with third-party platforms. These tools allow you to analyze charts, execute trades, and manage risk.

Platform Features You'll Need

- **Charting Tools:** Access to technical indicators, drawing tools, and multiple timeframes.
- **Order Execution Panel:** Fast trade entry options (market, limit, stop).

- **Level II Data / DOM (Depth of Market):** Useful for scalpers and short-term traders.
- **Trade Journal Integration:** Helps you track performance over time.

Building Your Chart Layout

A clean and functional chart layout is the heart of your trading station.

Recommended Layout:

- **Main Chart:** Price action on a 5-minute or 15-minute timeframe.
- **Secondary Chart:** Higher timeframe view (1-hour or daily).
- **Indicator Panel:** RSI, MACD, moving averages, or VWAP depending on your strategy.
- **Volume Profile or Footprint Chart (optional):** Advanced tools for analyzing order flow and price behavior.

Pro Tips for Chart Layout:

- Avoid clutter—keep only what you use.
- Use consistent colors for candles, indicators, and levels.
- Set alerts for key price levels or indicator signals.

Monitor Setup and Workspace

If you're serious about trading, consider investing in multiple monitors to improve visibility and efficiency.

Suggested Screen Usage:

- **Monitor 1:** Main trading chart and execution panel.
- **Monitor 2:** News feed, higher timeframe charts, or watchlist.
- **Monitor 3 (optional):** Trade journal, scanner, or DOM.

Summary

Your tools and setup are your command center. Choosing a trusted broker and building an efficient chart layout will give you the clarity and control needed to trade with discipline.

Key Takeaways

✔ Choose a futures broker with low fees, strong support, and solid platform reliability.

✔ Use a trading platform that includes customizable charts, fast execution, and trade journaling tools.

✔ Build a clean chart layout with the timeframes and indicators that support your trading strategy.

✔ A multi-monitor setup enhances focus and visibility, helping you stay on top of market action.

Chapter 4

Risk Management Fundamentals – Protecting Capital While Pursuing Profit

Introduction

Risk management is the cornerstone of long-term success in futures trading. While it may not be as exciting as chart patterns or trade execution, it is far more important. Without strict risk controls, even the best strategies will eventually fail. In this chapter, we'll break down the core principles of risk management, including how to limit losses, set proper stop levels, and manage position sizes with discipline.

Why Risk Management Matters

Every professional trader knows that preserving capital is more important than making profits. You can't grow an account that's constantly being drained by poor risk control.

Trading is a probability game: Losses are inevitable—even with a solid edge.

Survivability matters: Good risk management ensures you stay in the game long enough to see success.

Emotional control improves: Smaller, manageable losses reduce stress and impulsive behavior.

Position Sizing and Risk Per Trade

One of the simplest ways to manage risk is to control the amount you risk on each trade.

The 1% Rule (or Less)

- Never risk more than 1% of your total account balance on a single trade.
- For smaller accounts, consider 0.5% or even 0.25% to account for volatility.

How to Calculate Position Size

1. Determine your account size.
2. Decide your risk per trade (e.g., 1%).
3. Identify your stop-loss distance in ticks or points.
4. Use a position size calculator or formula:

Position Size = (Account Size × % Risk) / (Stop Loss in Ticks × Tick Value

Stop-Loss Strategy

Stop losses are not optional—they are your safety net.

Types of Stop Losses:

- **Hard Stops:** Fixed price levels where your trade will automatically close.
- **Trailing Stops:** Move with price action to lock in profit.
- **Mental Stops:** Used by experienced traders but risky for beginners.

Placing Your Stop:

- Base it on **market structure**, not arbitrary dollar amounts.
- Consider ATR (Average True Range) or recent support/resistance levels.
- Avoid placing stops where the market naturally wicks—this invites stop hunts.

Risk-to-Reward Ratio

Before entering any trade, ask yourself: *Is the potential reward worth the risk?*

Optimal R:R Ratio

- Aim for at least 2:1 (risking $1 to make $2).
- Scalpers may use 1.5:1 or even 1:1, but accuracy must be high.
- Swing traders should prioritize higher R:R, such as 3:1 or more.

Max Daily Loss Rule

Implement a rule that forces you to stop trading after hitting a certain loss threshold.

- Helps prevent revenge trading and emotional blow-ups.
- Example: Stop trading if down 3% of your account in one day.

Diversification and Correlation

While futures markets are less diverse than stocks, you can still reduce risk by understanding how assets are correlated.

- Don't trade multiple contracts that move together (e.g., CL and RB).
- Spreading risk across uncorrelated instruments can reduce volatility.

Summary

Risk management isn't about avoiding losses—it's about controlling them. Traders who focus on preservation over profits not only survive but thrive in the long run.

Key Takeaways

✔ Never risk more than 1% of your account on a single trade.

✔ Always use stop-losses based on structure, not emotions.

✔ Aim for a positive risk-to-reward ratio with every setup.

✔ Set daily max loss limits to prevent emotional decision-making.

✔ Understand market correlations to avoid overexposure.

Chapter 5

Developing the Trader's Mindset – Emotional Control and Discipline for Beginners

Introduction

Mastering your mind is just as important as mastering the charts. The best strategy in the world will fail if you can't execute it with discipline and emotional control. In this chapter, we'll explore the foundational elements of trading psychology and teach you how to build the mental resilience necessary to thrive in futures markets.

Why Trading Psychology Matters

Emotions like fear, greed, and frustration are natural—but they're also dangerous if left unchecked.

- **Greed leads to overtrading or oversizing.**
- **Fear causes hesitation and missed opportunities.**
- **Frustration can trigger revenge trading and account blowups.**

Your goal as a trader is not to eliminate emotion—but to manage it and prevent it from influencing decisions.

Building Emotional Discipline

Discipline means sticking to your plan no matter how you feel in the moment.

Daily Habits That Build Discipline:

- **Pre-market routine:** Start each session with a structured plan.
- **Journal your trades:** Capture not just the outcome, but the emotion behind it.
- **Follow your rules:** Execute based on your strategy, not your gut.

Consistency over time builds confidence, and confidence makes discipline easier.

Common Emotional Pitfalls and How to Avoid Them

1. Revenge Trading

Trying to make back losses by jumping into new trades impulsively.

Solution: Walk away after a max loss or bad trade. Take a breather to reset.

2. Fear of Missing Out (FOMO)

Chasing late entries or setups that don't meet your criteria.

Solution: Trust that the market will give you another opportunity. Missed trades are better than forced trades.

3. Overconfidence

Winning streaks can lead to carelessness or oversized positions.

Solution: Stick to your plan regardless of recent performance. Don't let wins override discipline.

Creating a Performance Routine

The best traders treat this like a profession—not a hobby.

Key Components of a Trading Routine:

- **Morning Prep:** Review key levels, news, and your trade plan.
- **Midday Review:** Evaluate performance so far—what's working or not?
- **Post-Market Reflection:** Analyze your trades and document emotions, mistakes, and wins.

Using Affirmations and Mental Cues

Simple, intentional phrases can help keep you grounded:

- "I only take trades that match my plan."
- "Losses are part of the game—I manage them like a pro."
- "My job is to execute, not to predict."

Pair these with deep breathing or a visualization exercise to reset your mindset between trades.

Mindset for Beginners vs. Experienced Traders

New traders often believe that learning more will fix emotional struggles. But the real fix comes from **self-awareness and repetition**.

- Accept that losses will happen.
- Focus on process, not outcomes.
- Learn to detach emotionally from individual trades.

Summary

The strongest edge in trading is your mindset. By developing emotional control and building discipline from day one, you lay the foundation for a long, successful trading career.

Key Takeaways

✔ Emotions like fear, greed, and frustration are normal—but they must be managed.

✔ A solid pre-market and post-market routine builds consistency and confidence.

✔ Track not just your trades, but your emotions and decisions behind them.

✔ Use mental cues and affirmations to reset during stressful moments.

✔ Focus on process over profits—this is how lasting success is built.

Chapter 6

Creating Your First Futures Trading Strategy – Step-by-Step Guide

Introduction

If you want to succeed in trading futures, you can't rely on gut feelings or random guesses. You need a **clear, repeatable strategy**. In this chapter, we'll walk you through a step-by-step blueprint for building your first futures trading strategy—from identifying trade setups to managing risk and planning your exit.

Step 1: Choose a Market and Timeframe

Start by narrowing your focus to one or two futures markets. This helps you get familiar with the price behavior and volatility.

Popular Beginner-Friendly Markets:

- **Crude Oil (CL):** High volume and volatility.
- **E-mini S&P 500 (ES):** A good mix of liquidity and technical behavior.
- **Gold Futures (GC):** Often respects key levels and reacts to news.

Timeframes:

- **Intraday Traders:** 5-minute, 15-minute, or 1-hour charts.
- **Swing Traders:** 4-hour and daily charts.

Pick a timeframe that suits your schedule and risk tolerance.

Step 2: Define Your Entry Criteria

Your strategy should have **clear rules for entering trades**. These rules should be based on objective signals—not emotions.

Entry Examples:

- Breakout above resistance with high volume.
- Pullback to the 20 EMA with a bullish candlestick confirmation.
- RSI crosses below 30 then reverses upward.

Document exactly **what has to happen** before you open a trade.

Step 3: Set Stop Loss and Target Rules

Define how much you're willing to risk and where you'll take profits.

Common Approaches:

- **Risk-Reward Ratio:** Aim for at least 1:2 (risk $100 to make $200).
- **ATR-Based Stops:** Use the Average True Range to determine logical stop distance.
- **Support/Resistance-Based Targets:** Exit near key zones.

Having this mapped out **before entering the trade** prevents emotional decisions later.

Step 4: Add Filtering Rules

Use filters to avoid low-quality trades.

Examples of Filters:

- Only trade when the market is trending.
- Avoid entering trades near major news releases.
- Only trade between specific hours (e.g., 9:30 am – 11:30 am EST).

Filters keep your strategy focused and reduce false signals.

Step 5: Test and Refine the Strategy

Before going live, test your strategy on historical data and in a simulated account.

Testing Methods:

- **Backtesting:** Go through past charts and record results manually or with software.

- **Paper Trading:** Use a demo account to trade your strategy in real-time.

Track your results and tweak anything that doesn't work consistently.

Step 6: Create a Trading Plan Document

Write everything down. Your trading plan is your rulebook—it keeps you disciplined.

What to Include:

- Market(s) traded
- Timeframe
- Entry rules
- Exit rules
- Risk management
- Daily routine and checklist

Print it. Follow it. Improve it over time.

Summary

You don't need a complex algorithm to make consistent profits—you just need a **defined strategy** that you understand and trust. Start small, stay disciplined, and grow as you learn.

Key Takeaways

✔ Focus on one or two markets to build familiarity and consistency.

✔ Define your entry and exit rules clearly, including stop loss and target placement.

✔ Use filters to improve the quality of your setups.

✔ Backtest and paper trade before risking real money.

✔ Document your strategy in a written trading plan.

Chapter 7

Chart Patterns and Price Action – Reading the Market Like a Pro

Introduction

Understanding chart patterns and price action gives you a powerful edge as a futures trader. These tools allow you to "read the tape" and anticipate moves before they happen. In this chapter, we'll break down key chart patterns, candlestick formations, and price action techniques that help you spot high-probability setups in any futures market.

Why Price Action Matters

Price action tells the story of buyers vs. sellers in real time—without relying on indicators.

Benefits of Reading Price Action:

- No lag (unlike indicators)
- Works on all timeframes and markets
- Helps confirm or invalidate other signals

If you want precision entries and exits, price action is essential.

Key Reversal Candlestick Patterns

Candlestick formations give clues about potential turning points.

Top Reversal Patterns:

- **Pin Bar (Hammer or Shooting Star):** Long wick signals rejection of a price level.

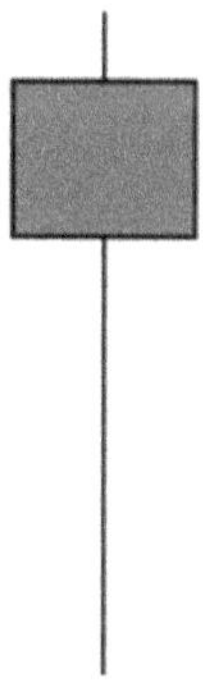

- **Engulfing Pattern:** Large candle "engulfs" the prior one—shows momentum shift.

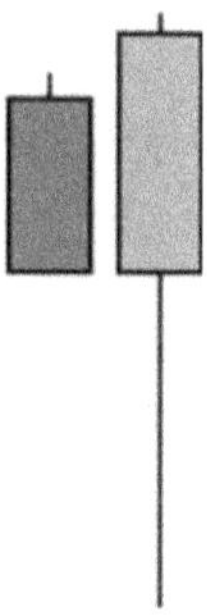

- **Doji:** Market indecision; potential reversal when found at key levels.

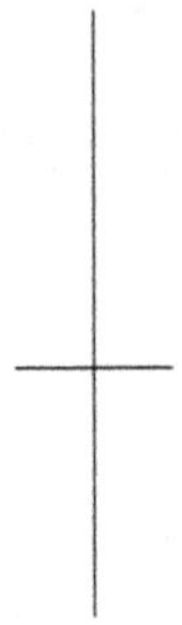

Continuation Candlestick Patterns

These patterns suggest a trend is likely to continue.

Examples:

- **Inside Bar:** Price consolidates—watch for breakout.

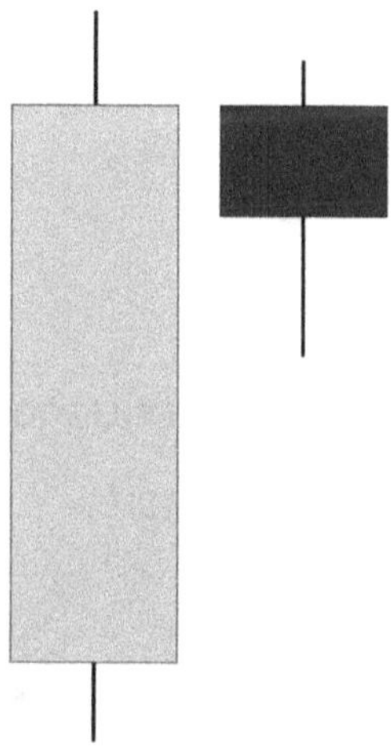

- **Bullish or Bearish Marubozu:** Strong momentum with no wicks.

- **Three-Bar Continuation:** Sequence of higher highs or lower lows with volume support.

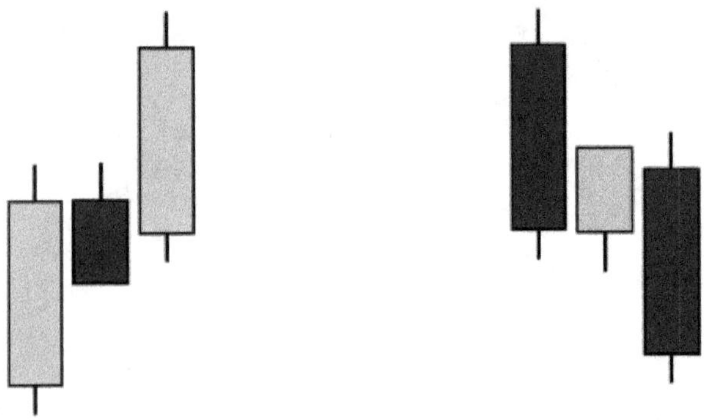

Classic Chart Patterns

These larger formations can signal breakouts or reversals.

Bullish Patterns:

- **Cup and Handle**
  - The Cup and Handle is a bullish continuation pattern that signals a potential breakout after a period of consolidation. It resembles the shape of a teacup on a chart—formed first by a rounded bottom (the "cup") followed by a smaller downward drift (the "handle"). This pattern typically forms during an uptrend and suggests that, after a brief pause, the price is ready to resume its upward movement.

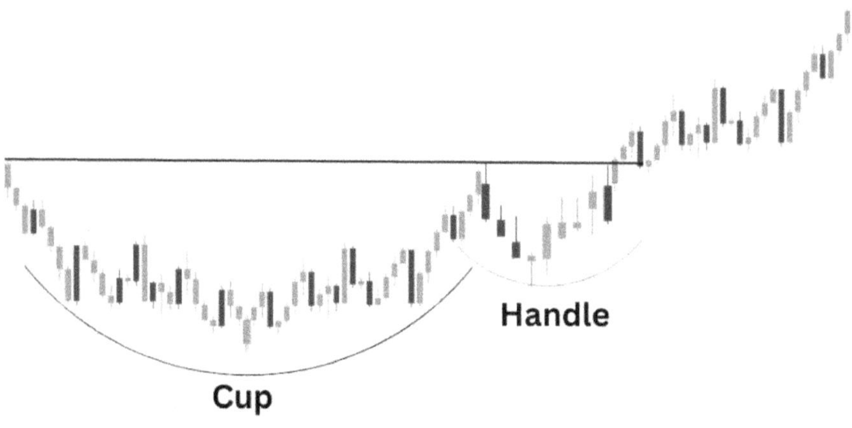

- **Ascending Triangle**
  - The Ascending Triangle is a bullish continuation pattern that forms during an uptrend and signals a potential breakout to the upside. It's defined by a horizontal resistance line at the top and a rising trendline at the bottom, indicating that buyers are gradually gaining strength and pressuring a breakout. This pattern reflects a buildup of buying pressure, and once resistance is broken, it often leads to a sharp upward move. Traders typically set targets by measuring the height of the triangle and projecting it upward from the breakout point.

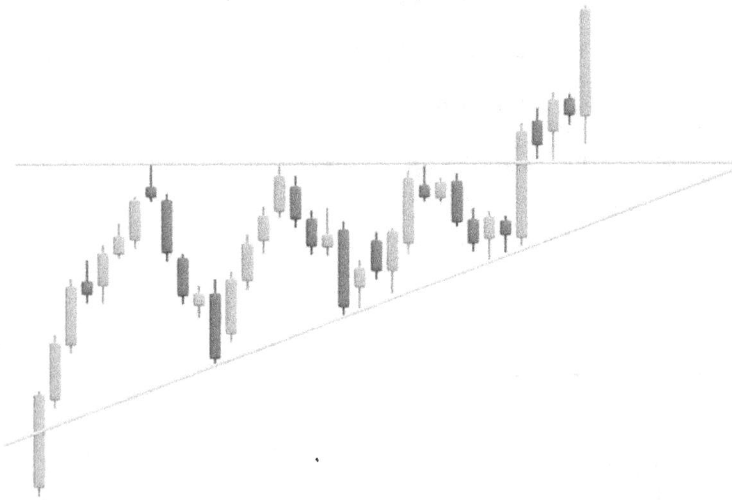

- **Double Bottom**
    - The Double Bottom is a powerful bullish reversal pattern that signals the potential end of a downtrend and the start of a new upward move. It is formed when price makes two nearly equal lows separated by a moderate peak, resembling the shape of a "W". This pattern reflects a shift in sentiment from bearish to bullish and is often followed by strong upward momentum. Traders commonly set profit targets by measuring the distance between the bottoms and the intervening peak and projecting it upward from the breakout level.

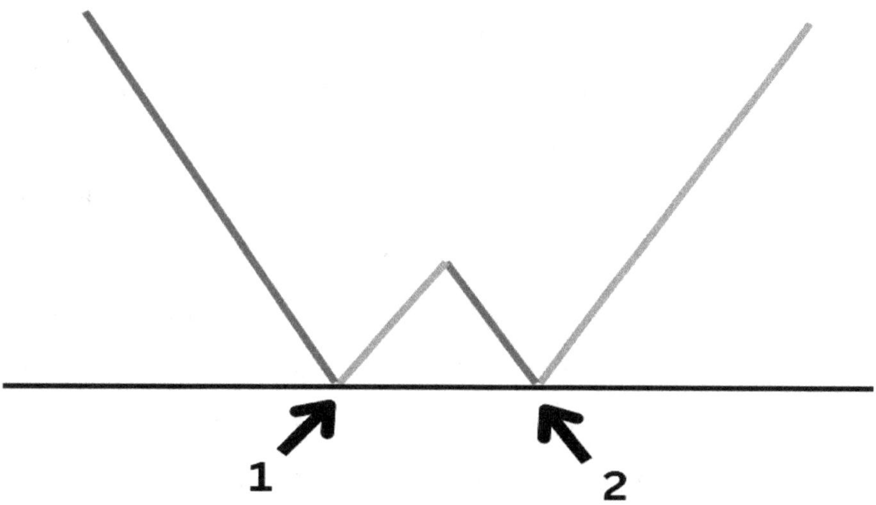

Bearish Patterns:

- **Head and Shoulders**
    - The Head and Shoulders is one of the most reliable bearish reversal patterns in technical analysis. It signals a potential trend change from bullish to bearish and forms after an extended uptrend. The pattern is defined by three peaks:
        - **Left Shoulder:** The first peak forms as the market rallies and then pulls back. This is a normal bullish swing.
        - **Head:** The price then makes a higher peak, forming the "head" of the pattern. This shows strong bullish continuation—temporarily.
        - **Right Shoulder:** After pulling back from the head, price makes a lower peak roughly equal to the left shoulder, indicating weakening buying pressure.
        - **Neckline:** A trendline drawn connecting the two swing lows between the shoulders and the head. It serves as the key support level.
    - The pattern is confirmed when price breaks below the neckline, signaling that the prior uptrend has likely ended. Volume often increases on the breakdown, strengthening the signal. Traders

often project the pattern's height (from the head to the neckline) downward from the breakout to set a profit target.

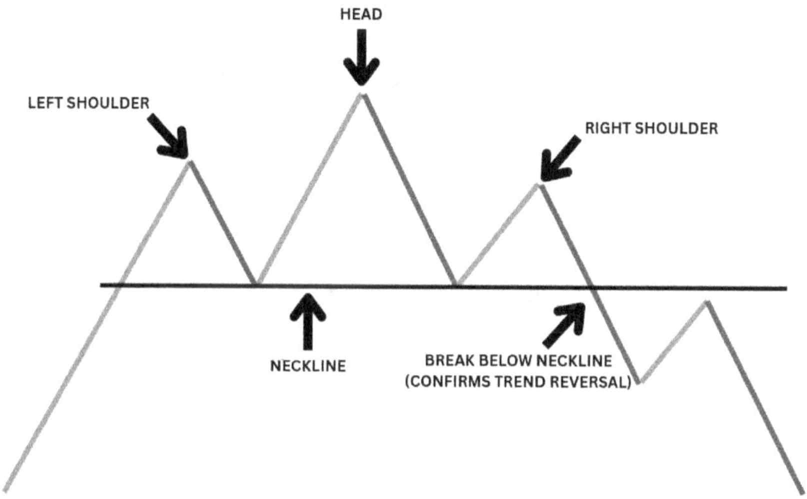

- **Descending Triangle**
  - The Descending Triangle is a bearish continuation pattern that typically forms during a downtrend, signaling that sellers are gaining strength and a breakdown may be imminent. It's characterized by a series of lower highs and a flat support level. The pattern is confirmed when price breaks below the horizontal support line with increased volume. This breakdown often signals the continuation of the prevailing downtrend. Traders typically project the triangle's height from the breakdown point to set profit targets.

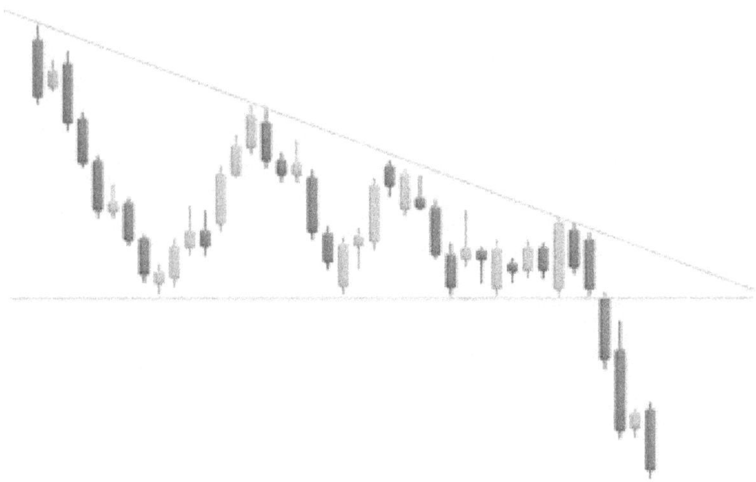

- **Double Top**
    - The Double Top is a classic bearish reversal pattern that forms after an extended uptrend, signaling that buying momentum is weakening and a trend reversal may be underway. The Double Top reflects a failed attempt by buyers to push the price higher a second time. Once support is broken, traders often target a move equal to the height of the pattern, measured from the tops down to the neckline.

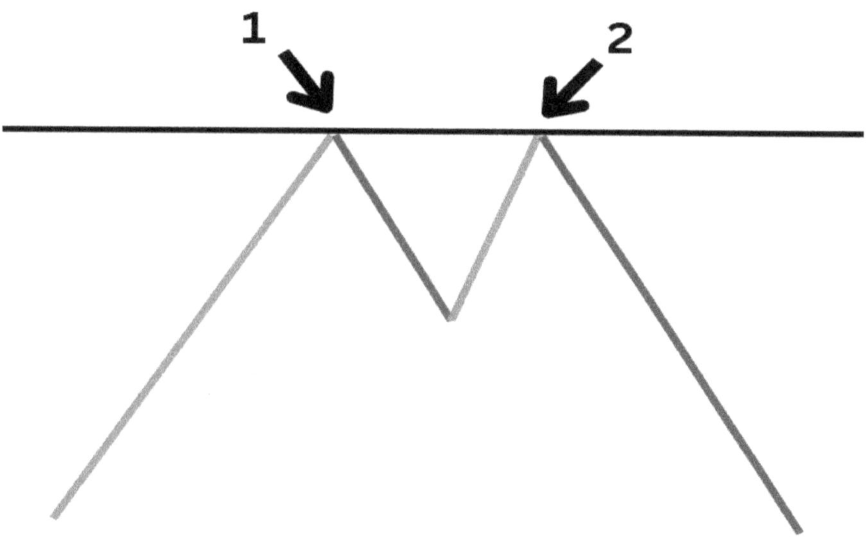

How to Use Support and Resistance

Support and resistance are price zones where buying or selling pressure tends to emerge.

How to Spot Support and Resistance:

- Look for horizontal levels that have been tested multiple times.
- Use previous highs/lows and high volume clusters.

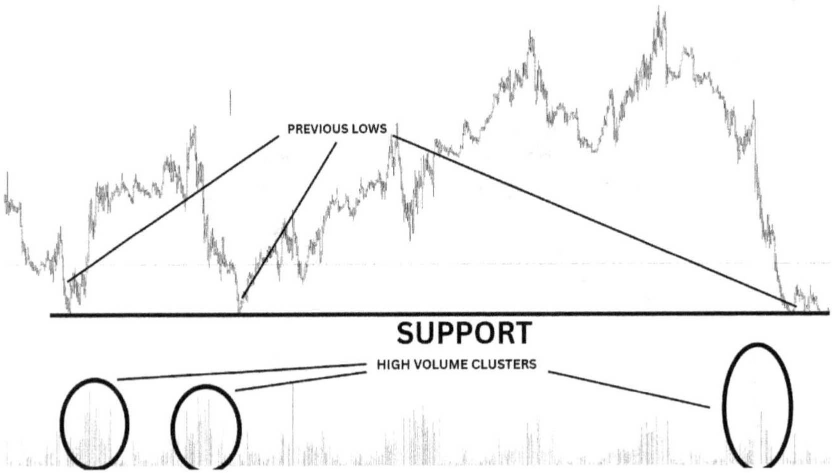

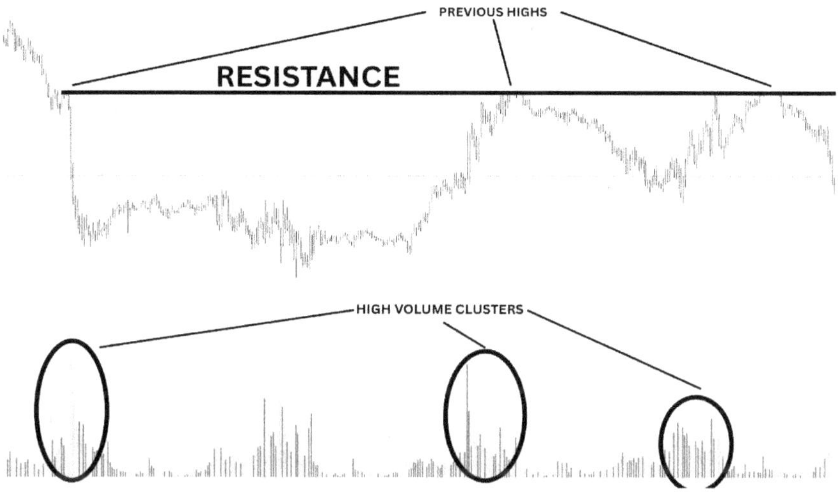

Best Uses:

- **Bounce Trades**
    - Buy near support or sell near resistance when price approaches these levels and shows signs of rejection (like reversal candlesticks or momentum fading).

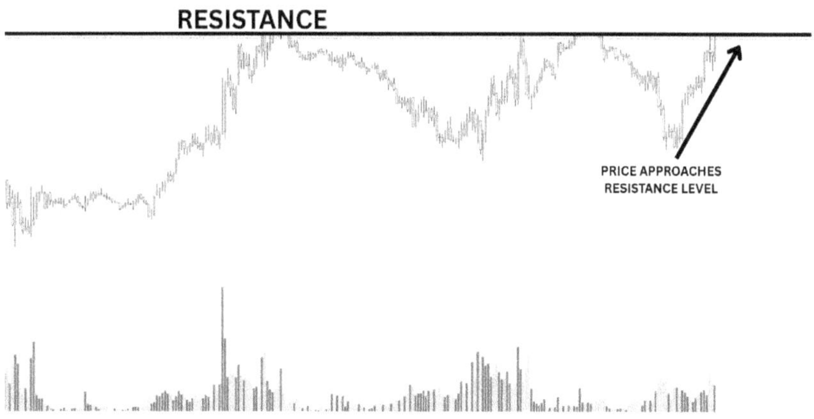

RESISTANCE
REVERSAL CANDLESTICK,
SELL HERE

RESISTANCE
ENTRY PRICE

- **Breakout Trades**
    - Enter trades when price breaks through a key level with strong volume and momentum.

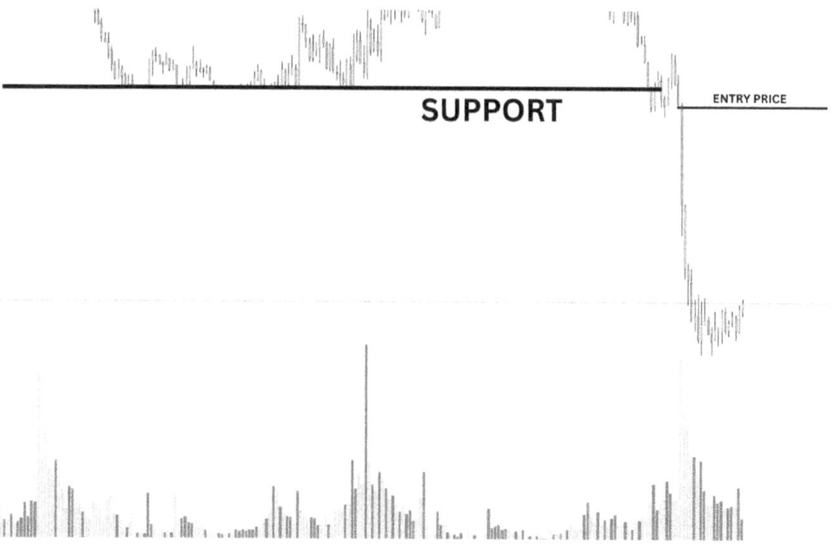

- **Stop-Loss Placement**
    - Place stops just below support for long trades or just above resistance for shorts to protect against false breakouts.

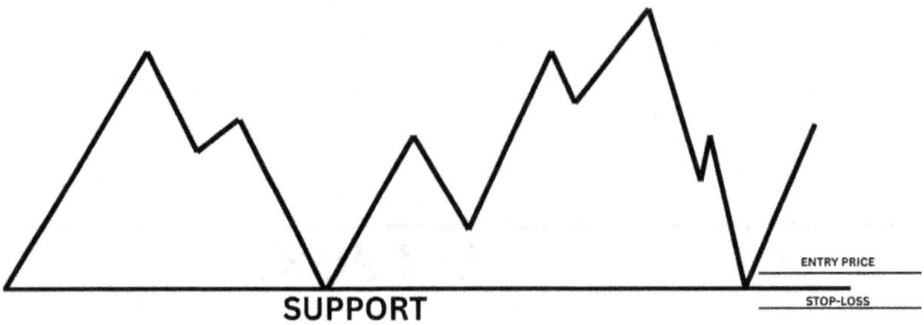

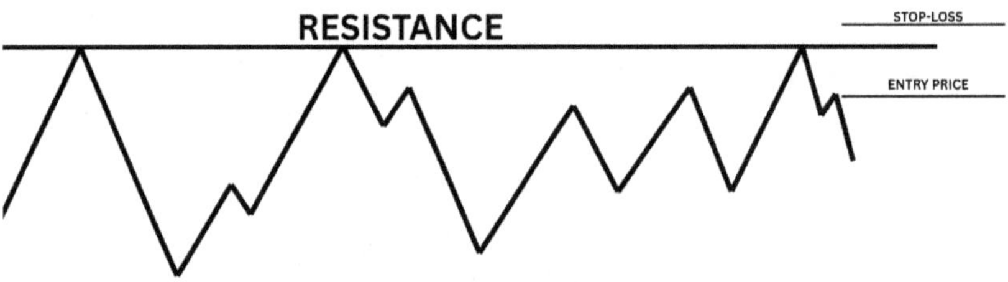

Building a Price Action Plan

Integrate these tools into your strategy by defining how you'll use them:

- Only take trades that show price rejecting a key level.
- Wait for confirmation from a candlestick pattern.
- Enter on breakouts from chart patterns with volume support.

Consistency comes from **applying the same rules over and over again**.

Summary

Mastering chart patterns and price action allows you to trade with clarity and confidence. You'll start seeing the market not as random—but as a structured environment with repeating behaviors.

Key Takeaways

✔ Price action gives you real-time insight into market momentum and structure.

✔ Reversal and continuation candlestick patterns can signal entry and exit points.

✔ Chart patterns like double tops, triangles, and head & shoulders often precede big moves.

✔ Support and resistance zones are critical areas to watch for reactions and breakouts.

✔ Combine patterns, context, and volume for high-probability trading decisions.

Chapter 8

Mastering Technical Indicators – The Ultimate Guide to Futures Trading Tools

Introduction

Technical indicators are the lifeblood of a futures trader's decision-making process. They help you time entries, confirm market direction, and manage risk with clarity. But not all indicators are created equal—and overusing them can cloud your judgment instead of sharpening it. In this chapter, we'll take a deep dive into the most powerful and widely used indicators that professional futures traders rely on to build winning strategies. You'll learn how each one works, how to use them in combination, and how to apply them to real futures contracts like oil (CL), gold (GC), and the S&P 500 (ES).

Why Indicators Matter in Futures Trading

Futures markets are fast-moving and highly liquid. That's great for short-term opportunities—but it also means split-second decisions. Technical indicators give you an edge by making market behavior more measurable and easier to interpret.

Key reasons traders use indicators:

- Confirm price trends or reversals
- Identify momentum and volume strength
- Signal overbought/oversold conditions
- Support entry, exit, and stop-loss placement
- Build confidence through data-based confirmation

Indicator #1: Moving Averages (MA)

What It Is:

A moving average smooths out price data to reveal the underlying trend direction over a selected time period.

Best Uses:

- **Trend confirmation (long-term MAs)**
    - If price is above the long-term MA, price is considered to be in an uptrend.

- If price is below the long-term MA, price is considered to be in a downtrend.

- **Dynamic support/resistance (short-term MAs)**
    - When price is in an uptrend, it will often pull back down to the short-term MA, before continuing higher.

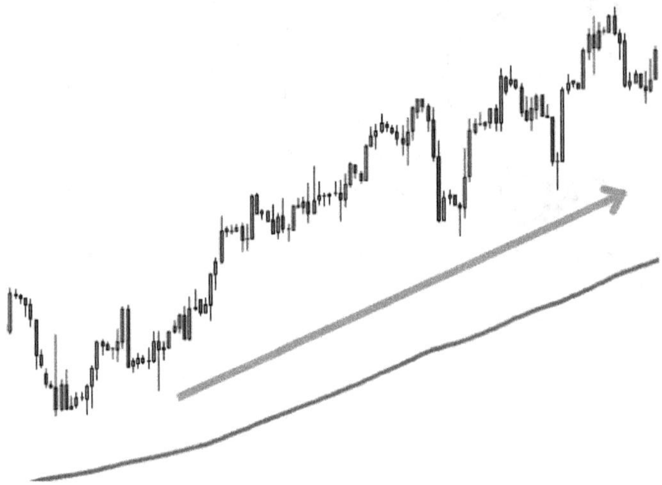

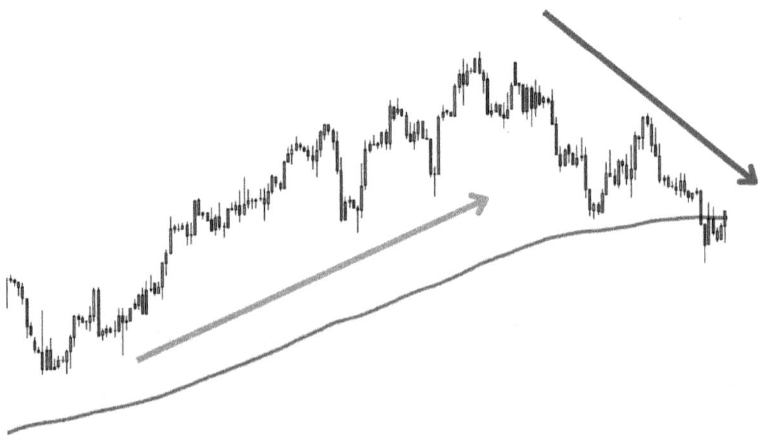

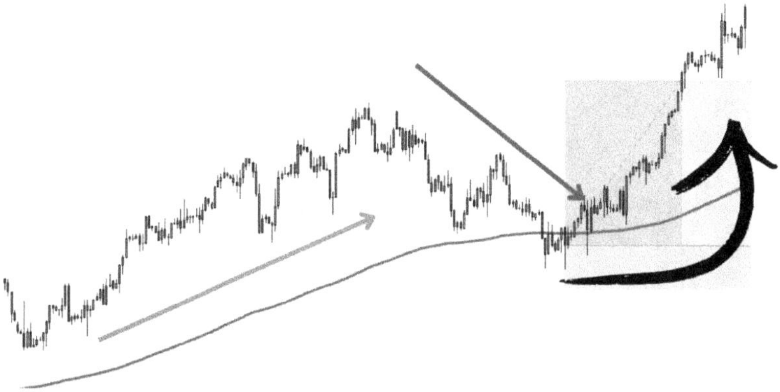

- When price is in a downtrend, it will often pull back up to the short-term MA, before continuing lower.

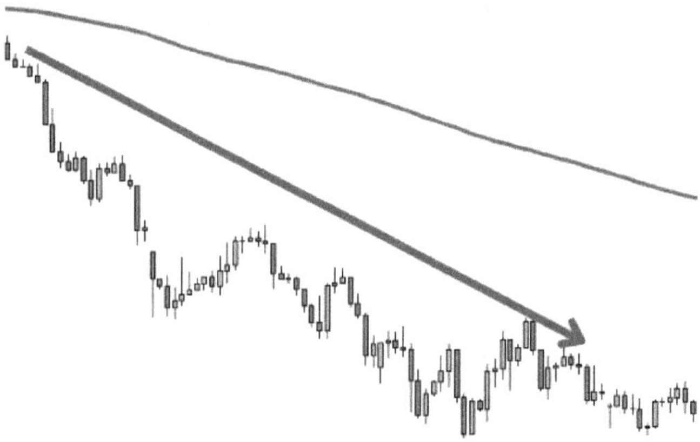

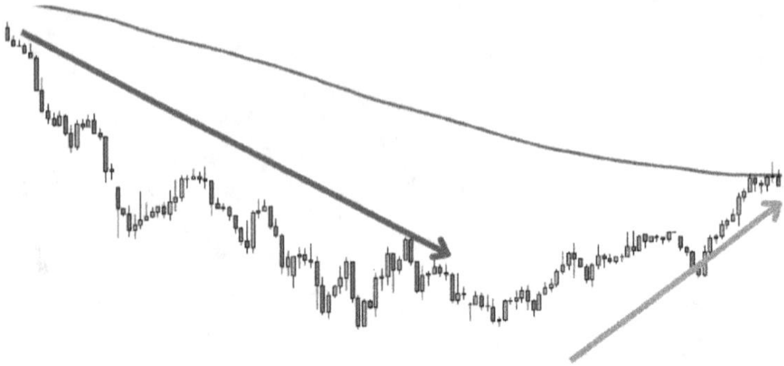

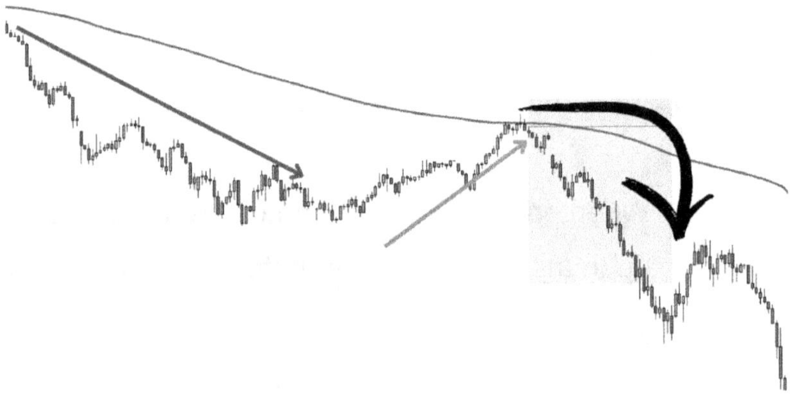

- **Crossovers for entries (e.g., 9 MA crossing above 21 MA)**
    - When price is in an uptrend, the shorter term MA like the 9 MA will often pull back below the longer term MA like the 21 MA, this signals that momentum upwards is fading and a potential reversal to the downside.

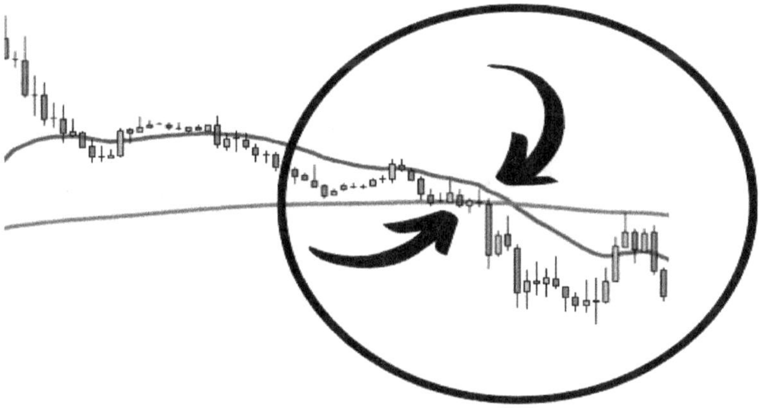

- When price is in a downtrend, the shorter term MA like the 9 MA will often pull back above the longer term MA like the 21 MA, this signals that momentum downwards is fading and a potential reversal to the upside.

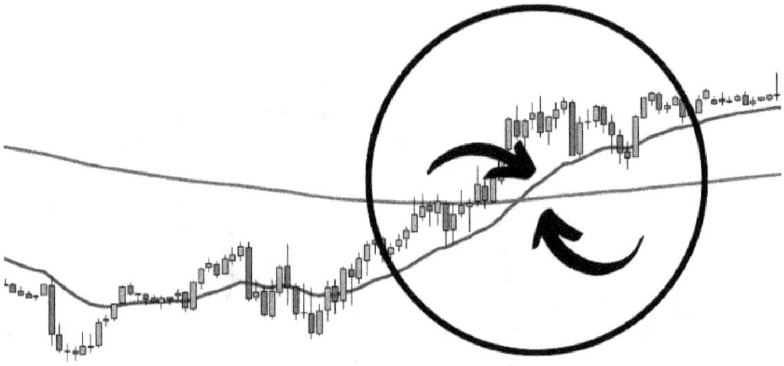

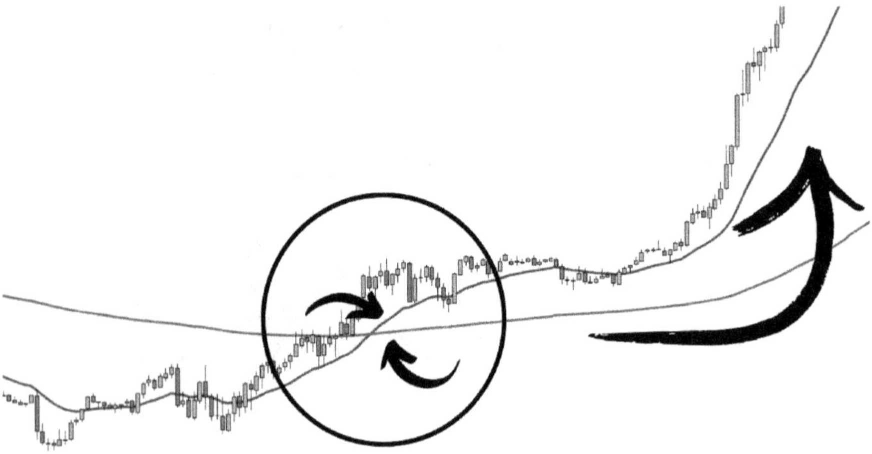

Pro Tips:

- Use the 50 EMA and 200 EMA to identify major market direction.
- Combine a fast (9 EMA) and slow (21 EMA) for a reliable crossover strategy.
- Apply on multiple timeframes to avoid false signals.

Indicator #2: Relative Strength Index (RSI)

What It Is:

RSI measures momentum and shows whether a market is overbought or oversold.

Key Levels:

- Overbought = Above 70
- Oversold = Below 30
- Neutral = Around 50

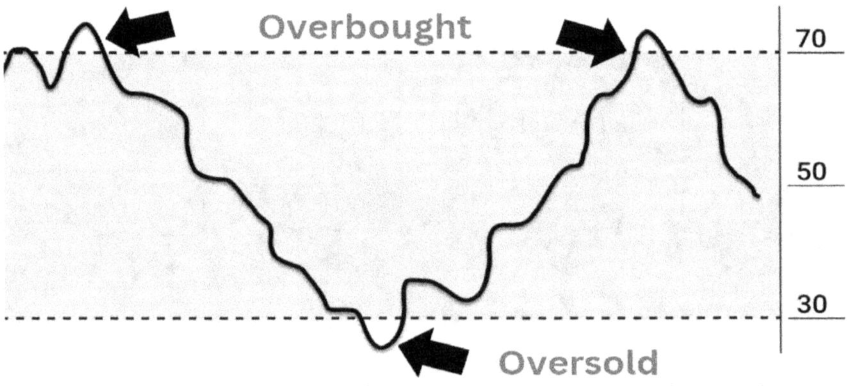

Best Uses:

- **Catching potential reversals**
    - When price is in a uptrend, RSI will often rise above 70 signaling the market is overbought and a potential downtrend reversal

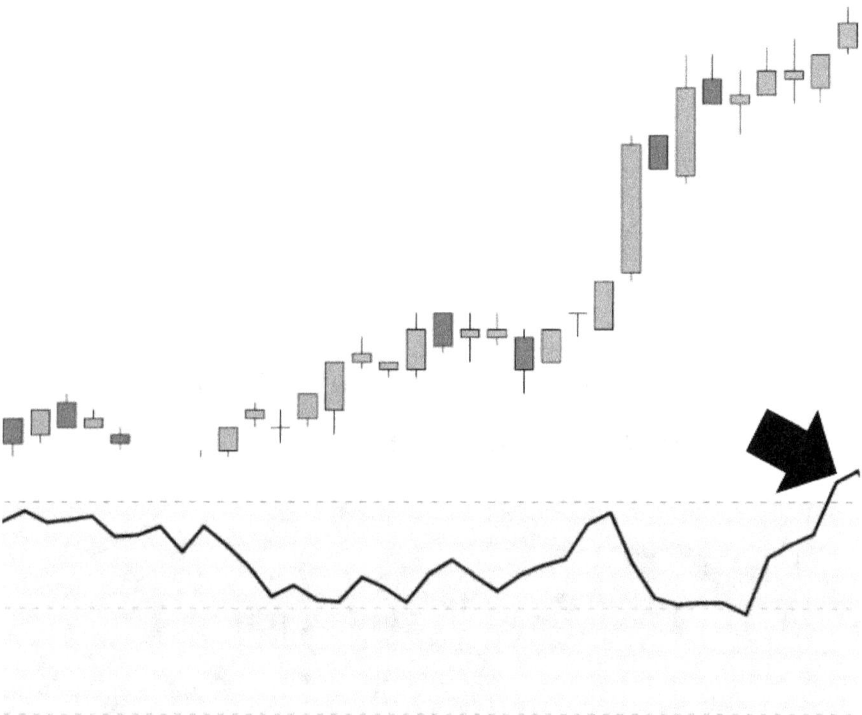

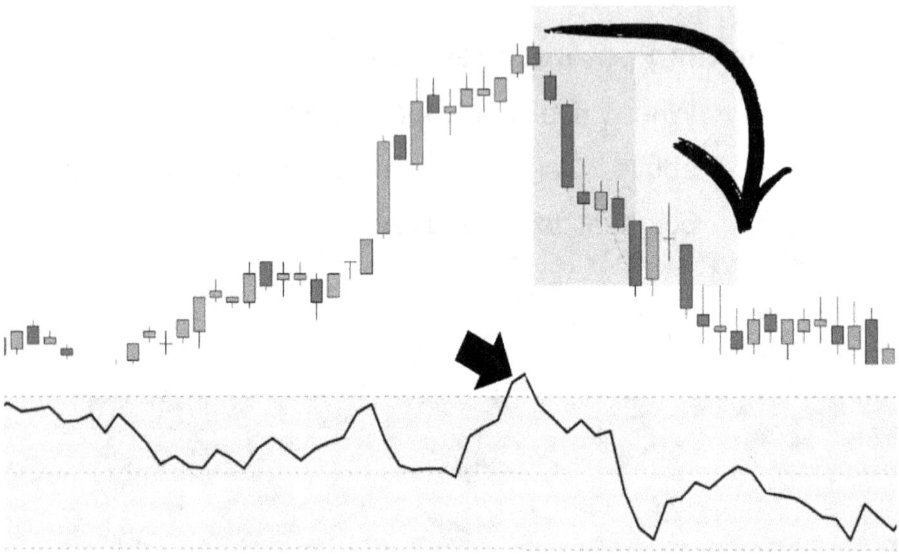

- When price is in a downtrend, RSI will often fall below 30 signaling the market is oversold

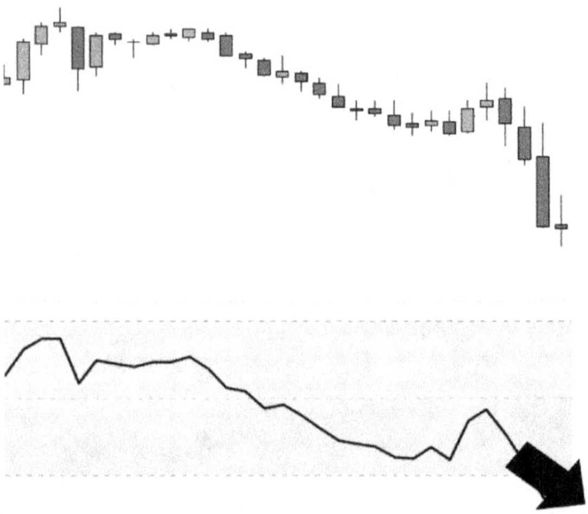

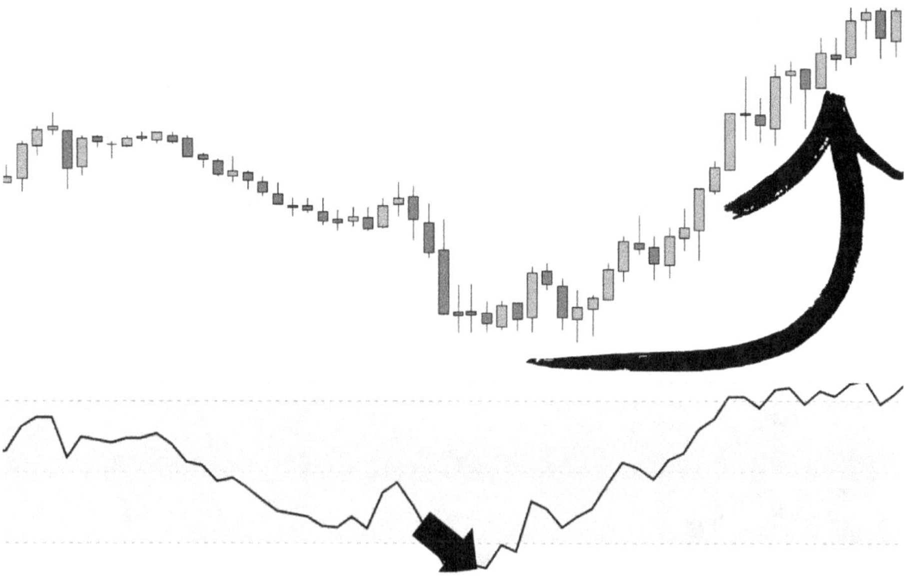

- **RSI divergences**
    - When price is making lower lows and lower highs, but RSI is making higher highs and higher lows, its signals that momentum downwards is fading and a potential reversal to the upside.

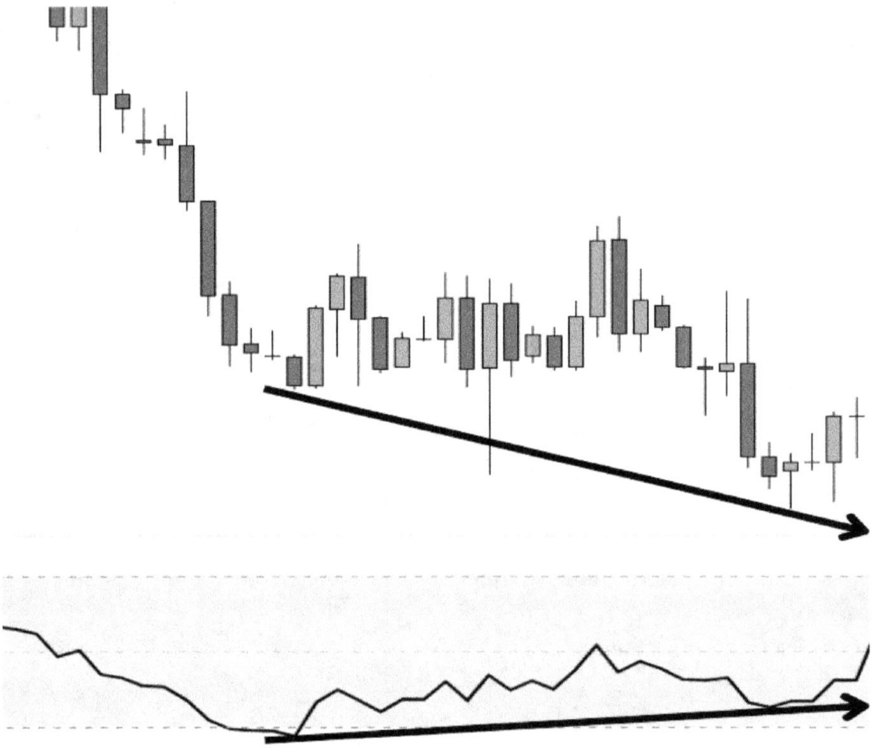

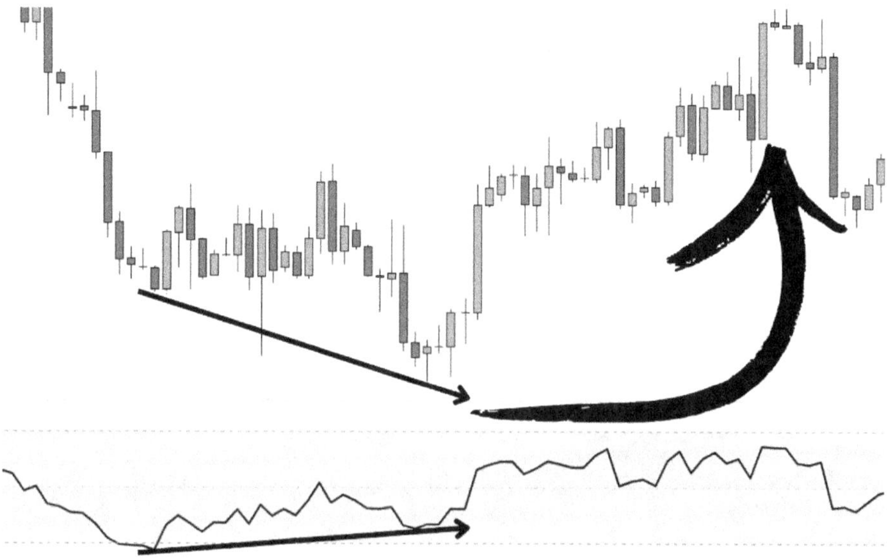

- When price is making higher highs and higher lows, but RSI is making lower lows and lower highs, it signals that momentum upwards is fading and a potential reversal to the downside.

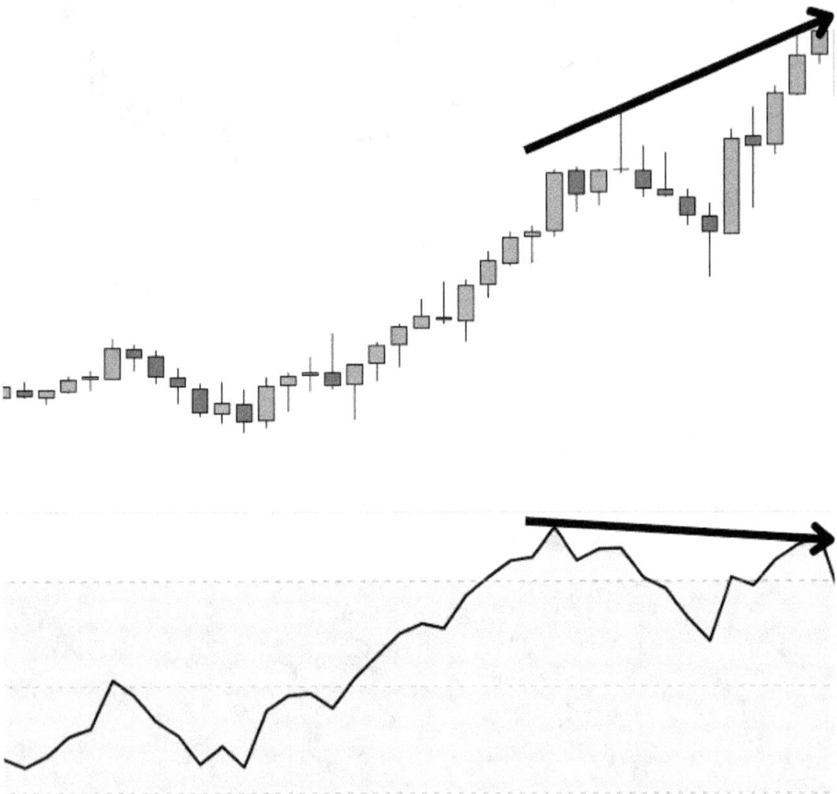

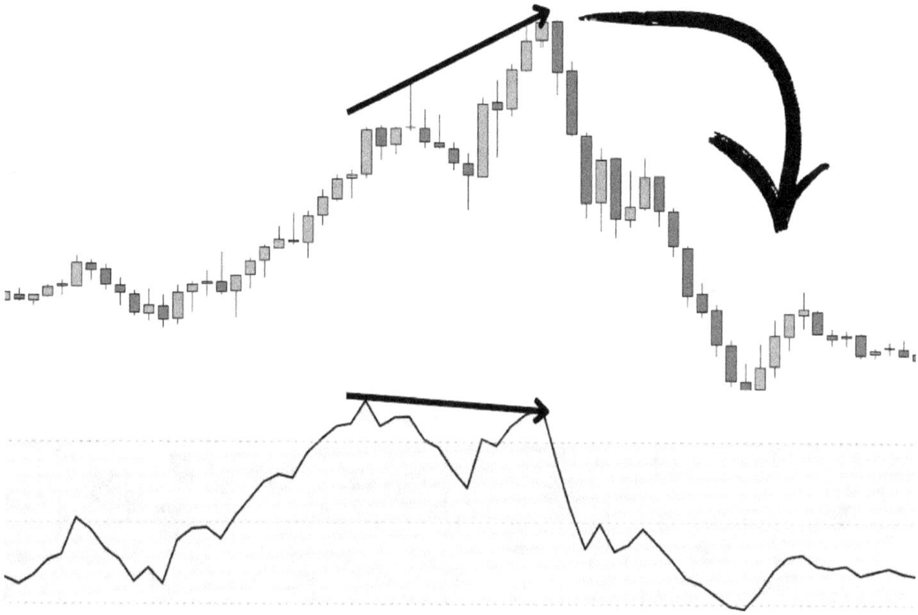

Pro Tips:

- Look for RSI divergences with price to spot turning points.
- Don’t use RSI alone—combine it with trend direction or support/resistance.

Indicator #3: Volume Profile

What It Is:

Volume Profile shows the volume traded at each price level over a selected time range. Unlike standard volume bars, it highlights *where* traders are most active.

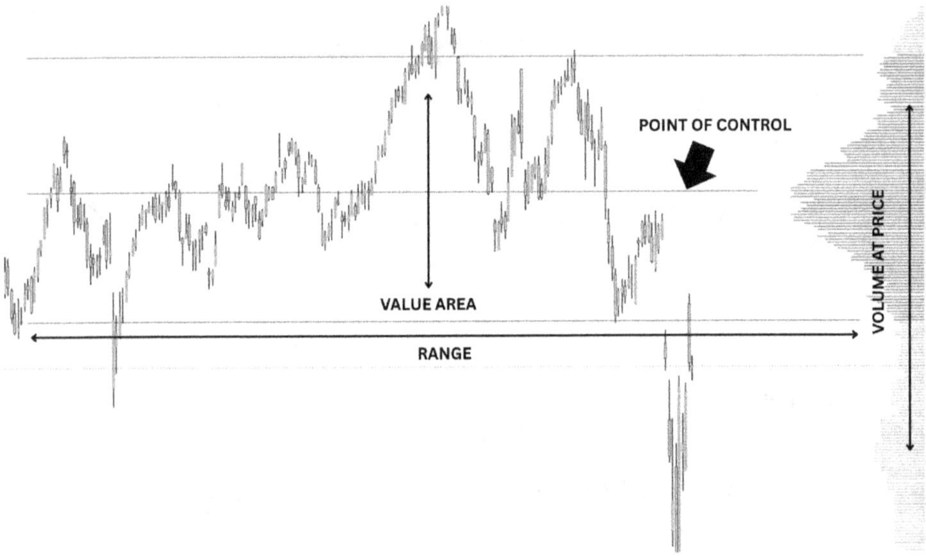

- **Point of control (POC)**
    - The longest volume bar in the range, this is the most traded price during the selected range.
- **Value area**
    - The price range where approximately 70% of all volume occurred during the selected time period.

Best Uses:

- **Spotting key support/resistance zones**
  - In an uptrend, price will often pull back down to, and bounce off of the point of control, before continuing higher.

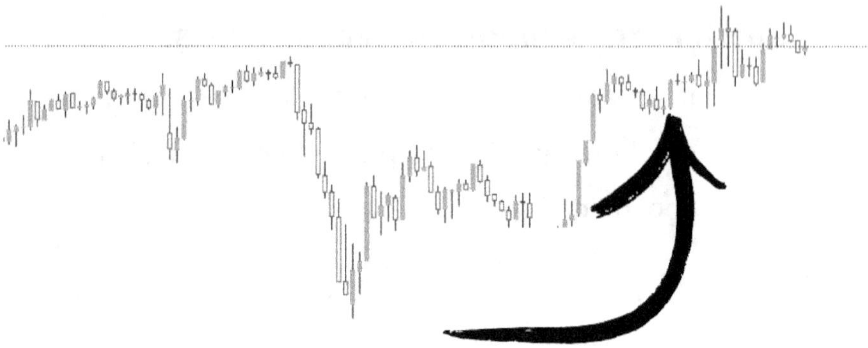

- In a downtrend, price will often pull back up to, and bounce off the point of control, before continuing lower.

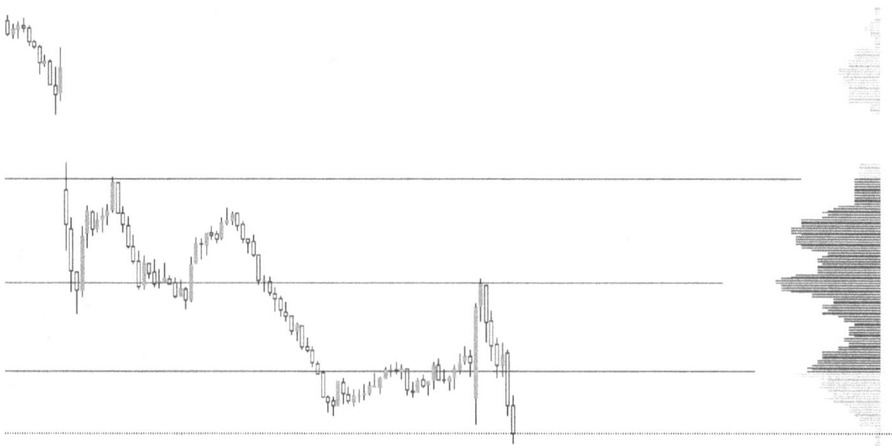

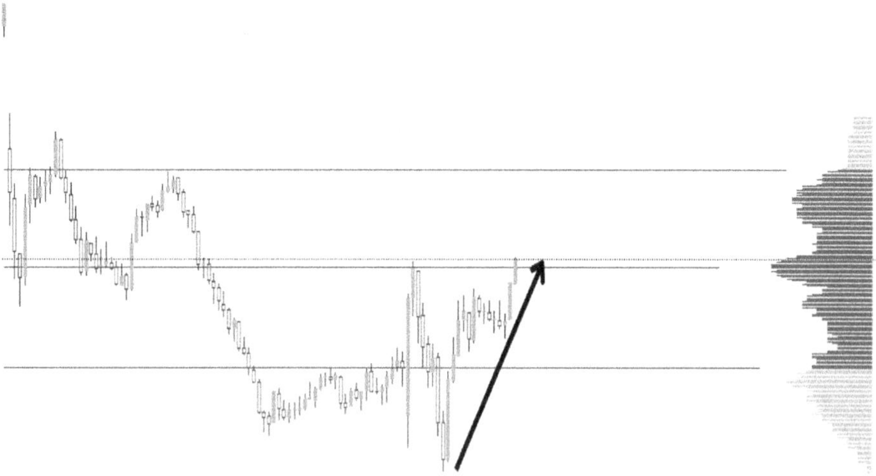

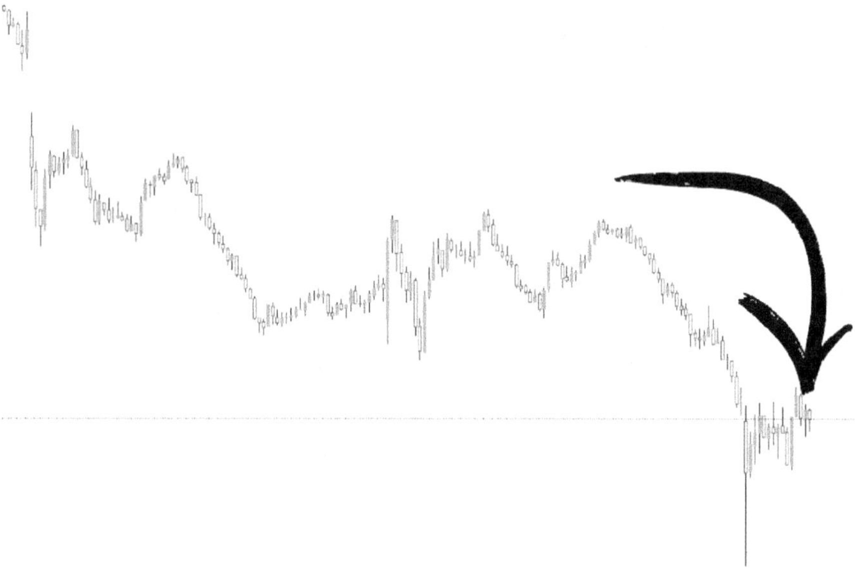

- **Identifying low-volume areas (price may move through quickly)**
    - Areas where there is low volume, signals there isn't much buying or selling pressure at that price, signaling that there could be weak support or resistance for price at that level.

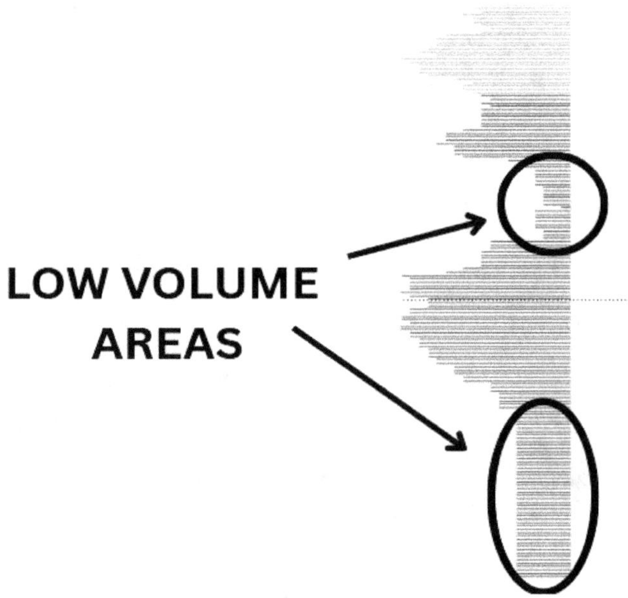

Pro Tips:

- Use to confirm breakout zones and trade around high-volume areas.

- Combine with candlestick confirmation for sniper entries.

Indicator #4: VWAP (Volume-Weighted Average Price)

What It Is:

VWAP tracks the average price a futures contract has traded at throughout the day, based on both volume and price.

Best Uses:

- **Benchmark for institutional price levels**
  - The VWAP is oftentimes used by institutional investors and traders to time their entries and exits.

- **Entries at support and resistance**
  - Similar to MA's, the VWAP can be used as support and resistance levels. When price is in an uptrend and above VWAP, it will often pull back down to the VWAP, before continuing higher.

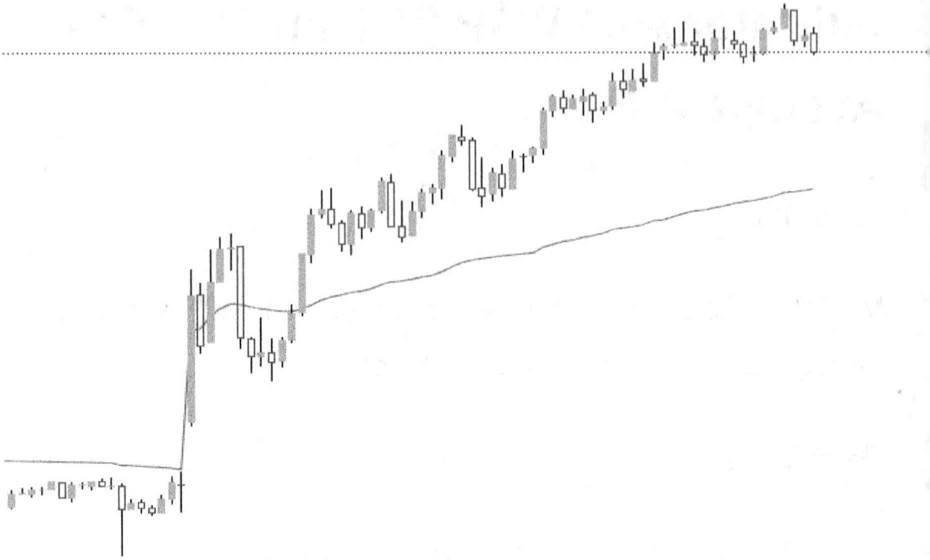

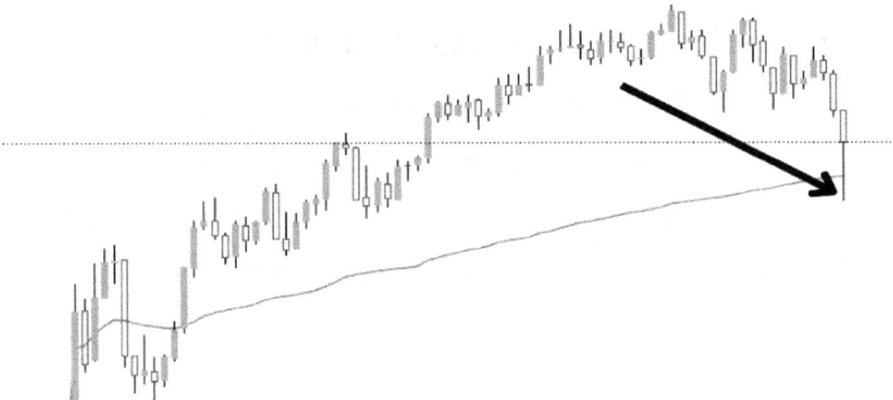

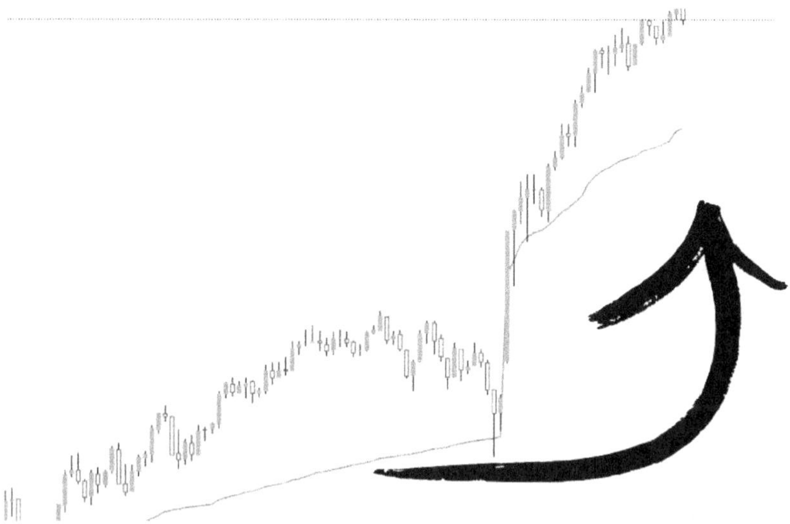

- When price is in a downtrend and below VWAP, it will often pull back up to the VWAP, before continuing lower.

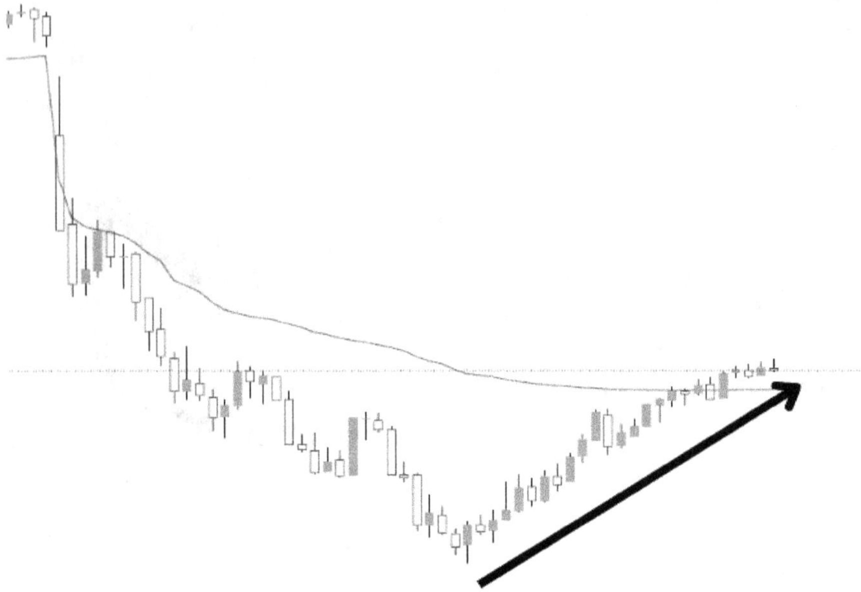

Pro Tips:

- Price above VWAP = bullish bias; below VWAP = bearish bias
- Excellent for identifying pullbacks in trending markets

Indicator #5: MACD (Moving Average Convergence Divergence)

What It Is:

MACD tracks trend direction and momentum by comparing two EMAs (commonly 12 and 26), plus a signal line.

Signals:

- MACD Line crossing Signal Line = entry signal
- MACD crossing zero line = trend confirmation

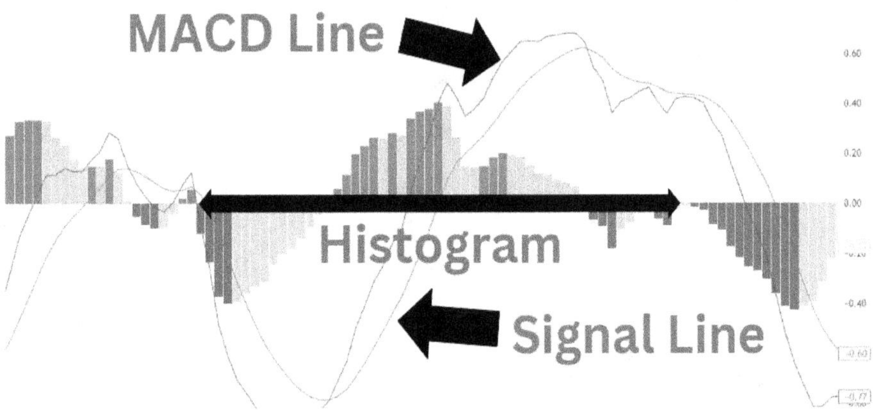

Best Uses:

- **Spotting trend reversals**
  - When price is in an uptrend, and the MACD line crosses below the signal line, it signals upward momentum is fading and a potential downwards reversal.

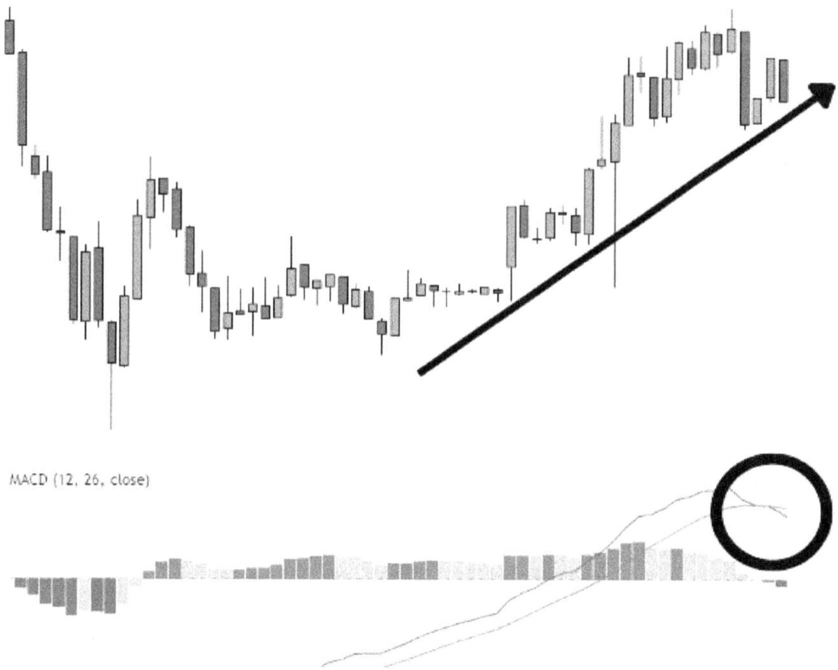

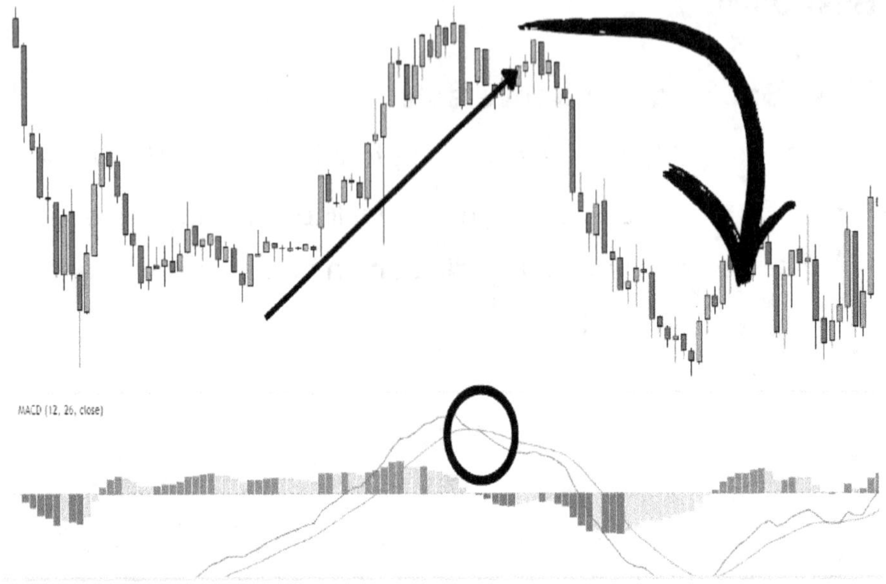
MACD (12, 26, close)

- When price is in a downtrend, and the MACD line crosses above the signal line, it signals downwards momentum is fading and a potential upside reversal.

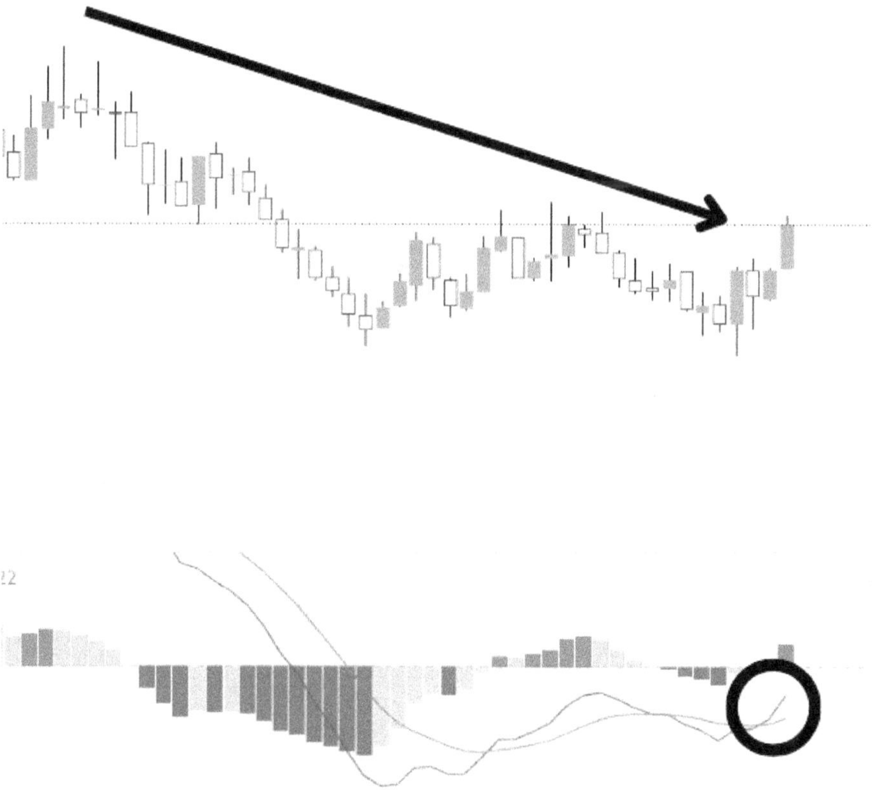

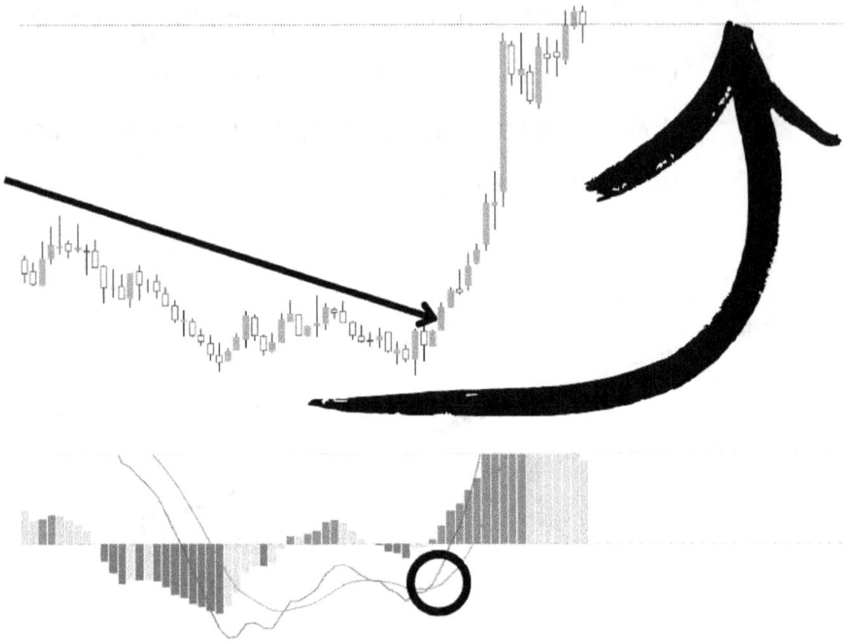

- **Trailing stop loss**
    - Using MACD crossovers is a great way to manage trades dynamically, based on momentum shifts. For long positions that are in profit, hold the position as long as the MACD line stays above the signal line. As soon as the MACD line crosses below the signal line, exit the position.

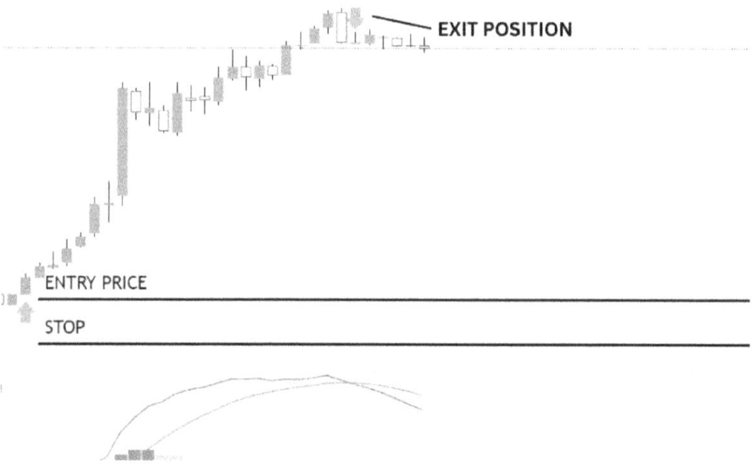

- For short positions that are in profit, hold the position as long as the MACD line stays below the signal line. As soon as the MACD line crosses above the signal line, exit the position.

Pro Tips:

- Works best on higher timeframes (15m, 1H+)
- Combine with RSI or price structure for cleaner setups

Indicator #6: Bollinger Bands

What It Is:

Bollinger Bands consist of a moving average (middle band) and two standard deviations above and below it.

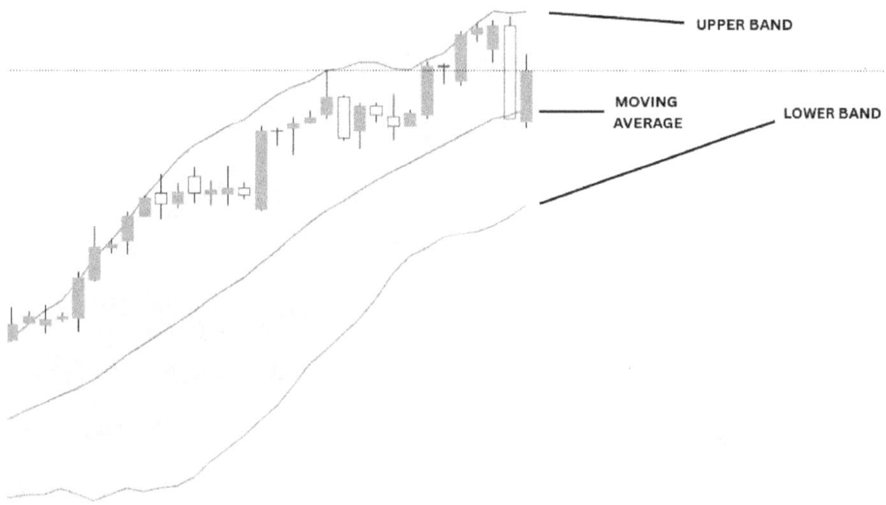

Middle Band: A 20-period simple moving average (SMA)

Upper Band: SMA + 2 standard deviations

Lower Band: SMA – 2 standard deviations

Best Uses:

- **Identify volatility squeezes and breakouts**
    - A volatility squeeze occurs when the bands contract tightly around the price, this shows a period of low volatility and consolidation — usually right before a sharp breakout. To identify volatility squeezes with bollinger bands, look for the narrowest bollinger band width in recent history.

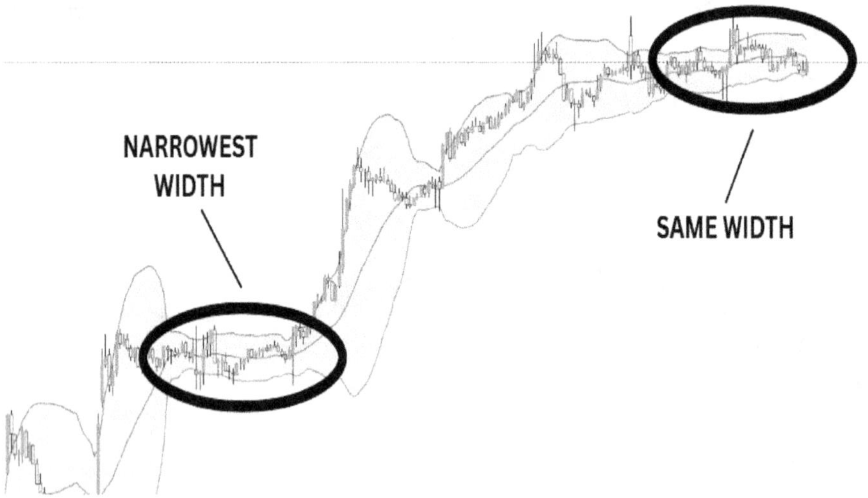

- To identify breakouts with bollinger bands, watch for a strong breakout candle that closes outside the upper or lower band. If price breaks above the upper band, there is bullish momentum and price will often breakout to the upside.

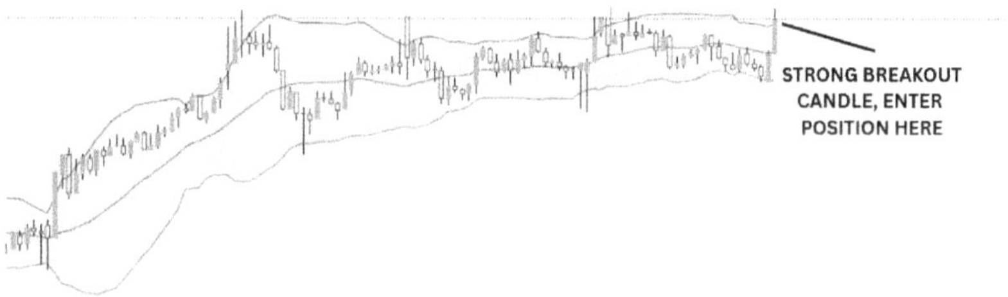

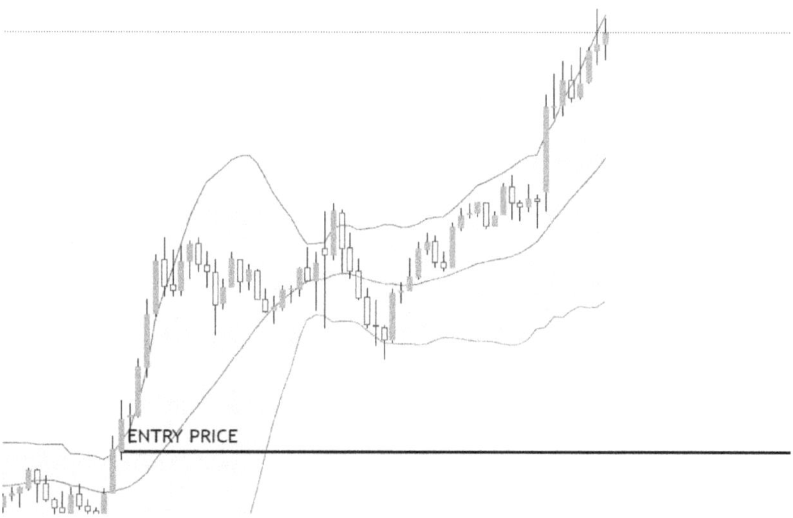

- If price breaks below the lower band, there is bearish momentum and price will often breakout to the downside.

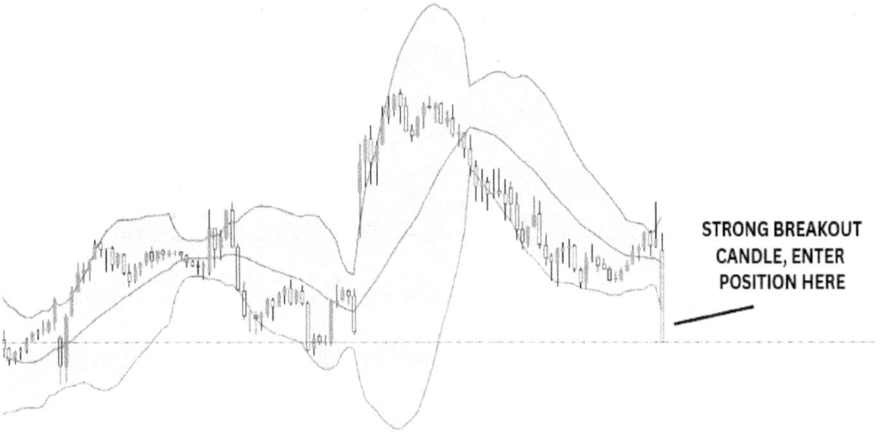

- **Catch mean reversion trades**
    - Mean reversion assumes that price tends to return to its average (the "mean") after moving too far in either direction. In Bollinger Bands, this "mean" is the 20-period simple moving average (SMA). The best time to use Bollinger Bands for mean reversion is when the market is moving sideways and not trending. When price hits the lower band, it's seen as oversold and there is a potential move to the upside.

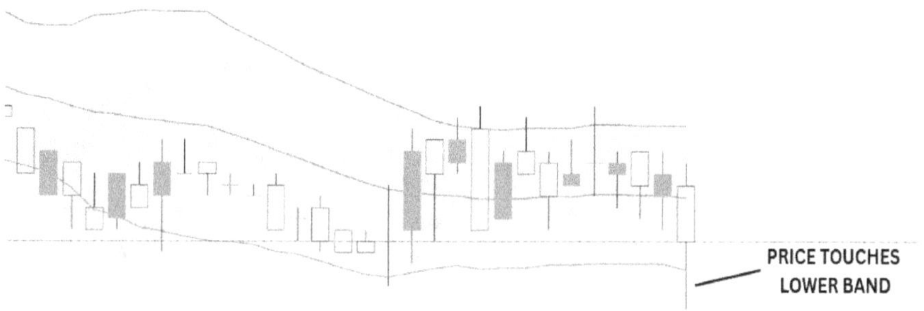

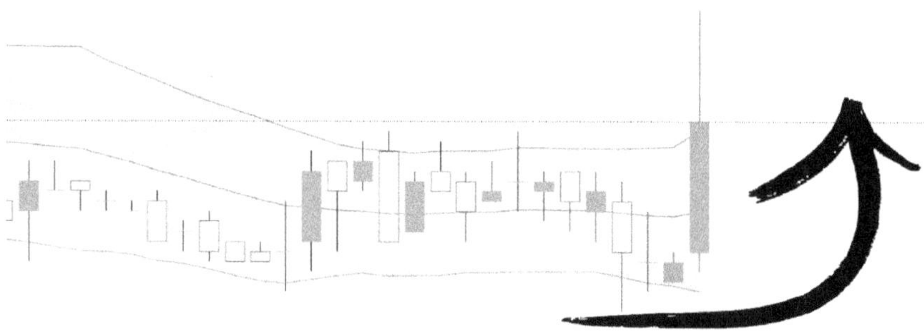

- When price hits the upper band, it's seen as overbought and there is a potential move to the downside.

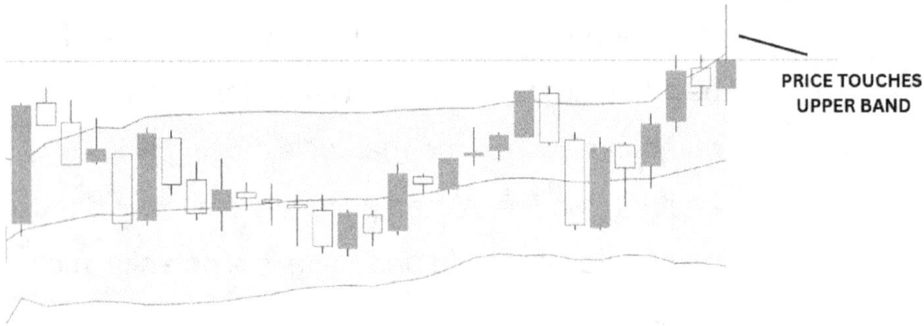

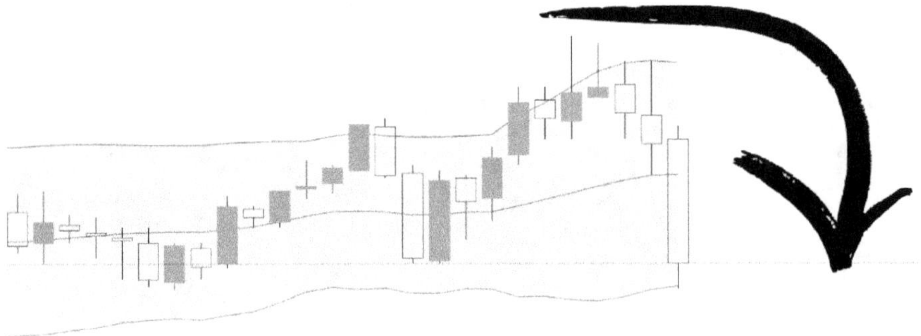

Pro Tips:

- Price touching upper band ≠ sell signal. Confirm with momentum.
- Look for "Bollinger Band squeezes" before strong directional moves.

Indicator #7: ATR (Average True Range)

What It Is:

ATR measures market volatility—not direction. It tells you how much a contract typically moves during a session.

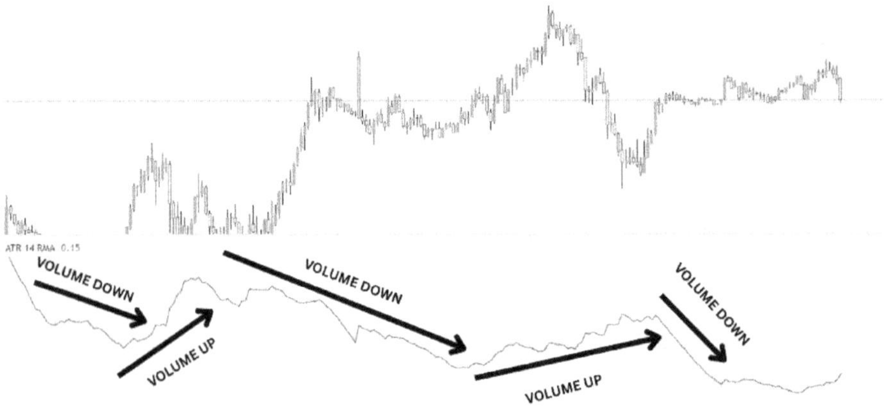

Best Uses:

- **ATR-Based Stop-Loss Setting**
  - Using the ATR as a tool to set your stop-loss helps avoid placing stops too tight (and getting stopped out by noise), it also helps with adapting to market volatility — in high-volatility markets, you give the trade more room; in low-volatility markets, you tighten up.

- To use the ATR to determine stop-loss placement multiply the current ATR value by 2 to determine how far your stop-loss should be.
- Ex. If the ATR is 0.15 on a 15-minute oil futures chart and you use a 2x ATR stop, place your stop 0.30 points away from your entry.

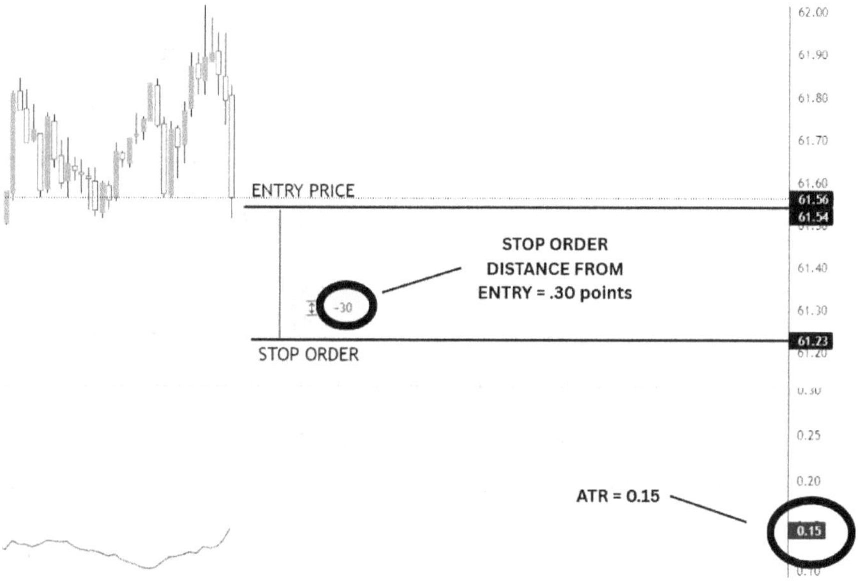

- **Position sizing**
    - Using the ATR for position sizing keeps your risk consistent, no matter how volatile the market is, it also helps with avoiding overleveraging in fast markets and under-sizing in calm ones.
    - To determine position sizing with the ATR, first determine your risk per trade. Secondly, calculate your stop distance – Use the ATR multiple (e.g., ATR = 0.25, stop = 0.50 points). Next, find the dollar value per tick/point. Lastly, plug everything into the position size formula, which is “position size = risk per trade / stop-loss in $”.
    - Ex. If your willing to risk $100 on a trade, the dollar value per tick/point is $100 and the stop distance is 1.0 point (ATR = 0.50, stop = 1.0 point), the position sizing formula would be “position size = 100 / 100 = 1 contract”. So on this trade, a position of 1 contract would risk $100 if the stop-loss order gets filled.

Pro Tips:

- Use 2x ATR as a guideline for swing trade stops.
- Combine ATR with trend indicators to refine entries.

Indicator #8: Stochastic Oscillator

What It Is:

A momentum indicator that compares a closing price to its price range over a specific period. The stochastic oscillator consists of 4 parts, first is the %K line, second is the %D line, next is the upper trigger line, and lastly is the lower trigger line.

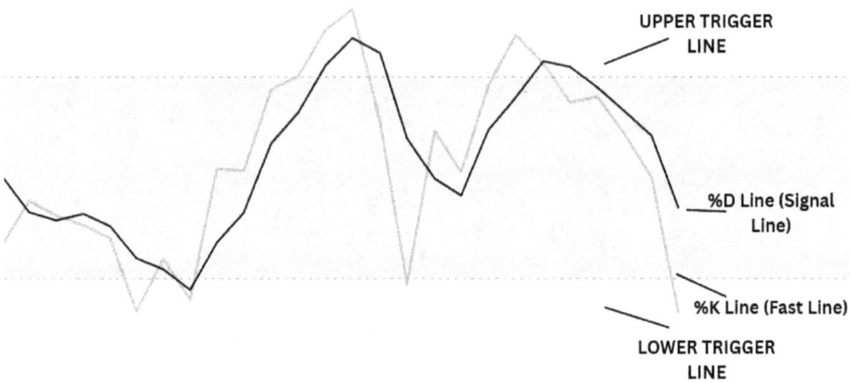

- %K Line (Fast Line): Measures the current closing price relative to the range (high-low) over a set period — typically 14 periods.
- %D Line (Signal Line): A 3-period simple moving average (SMA) of the %K line.
- Upper and lower trigger lines: Signals Overbought & Oversold Levels.

Best Uses:

- **Timing reversals in range-bound markets**
    - The stochastic oscillator is especially effective at timing reversals in range-bound markets because it identifies overbought and oversold conditions — key signals that a price move is likely to reverse within a sideways range.
    - To use the stochastic oscillator to determine reversals in range bound markets, first watch for overbought and oversold readings, then use %K line and %D line crossovers to confirm the incoming reversal. If the stochastic %K and %D are both above 80 signaling that price is overbought, and the %K line crosses below the %D line, upwards momentum is fading and there is a potential downwards reversal incoming.

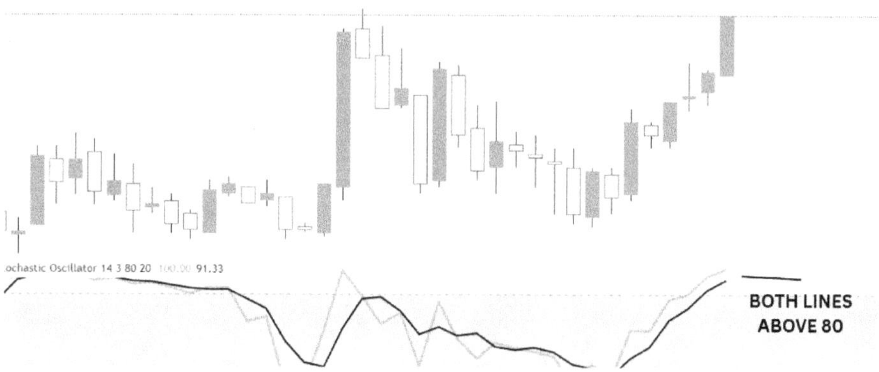

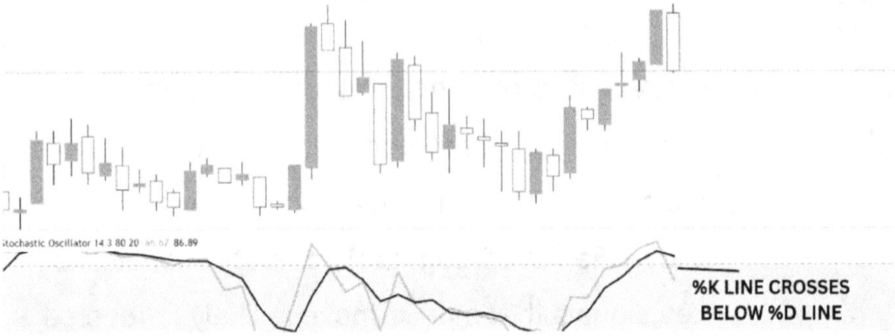
%K LINE CROSSES
BELOW %D LINE

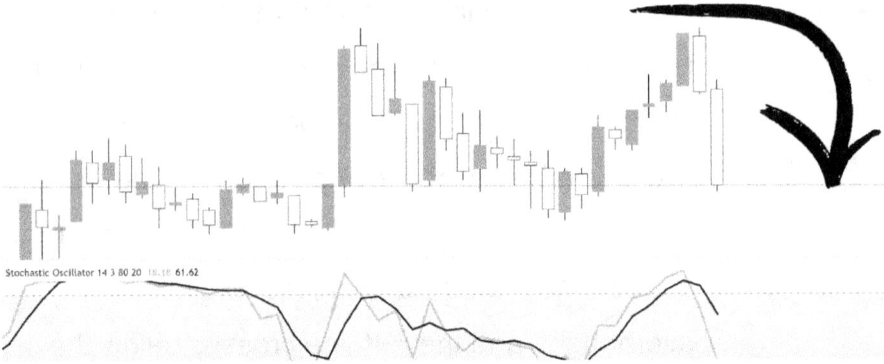
Stochastic Oscillator 14 3 80 20

- If the stochastic %K and %D are both below 30 signaling that price is oversold, and the %K line crosses above the %D line, downwards momentum is fading and there is a potential downwards reversal incoming.

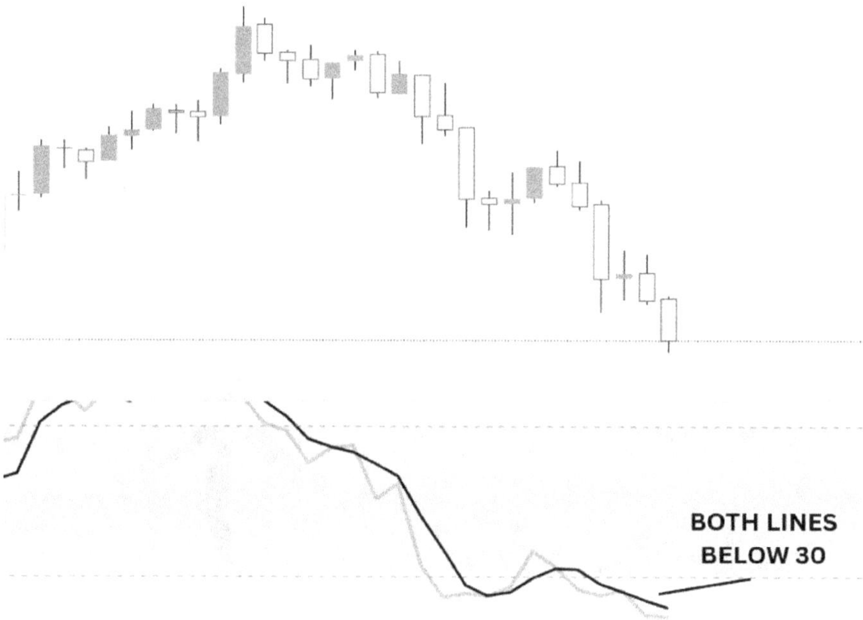

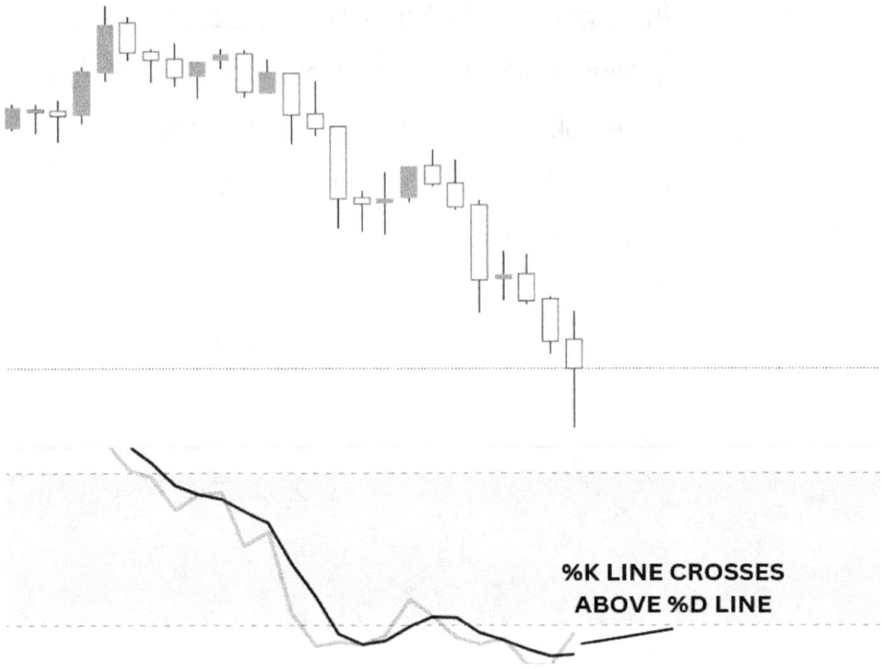
%K LINE CROSSES
ABOVE %D LINE

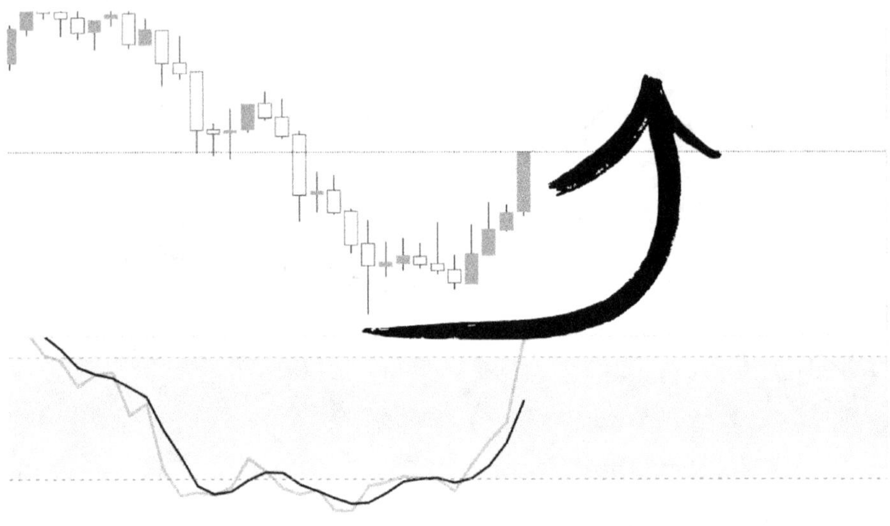

Pro Tips:

- Use in conjunction with support/resistance zones
- Wait for crossovers in extreme zones (above 80 or below 20)

How to Combine Indicators Effectively

No single indicator is perfect. In fact, relying on one can lead to false signals and bad trades. The power lies in *confluence*—when multiple indicators and price structure agree.

Smart Combinations:

- **Trend + Momentum**: Moving Averages + MACD

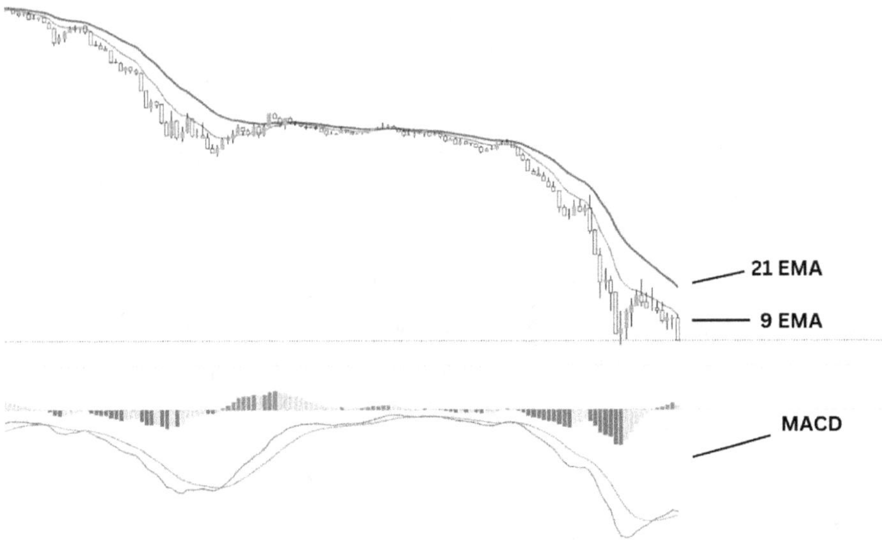

- **Breakout Confirmation**: Volume Profile + VWAP + RSI

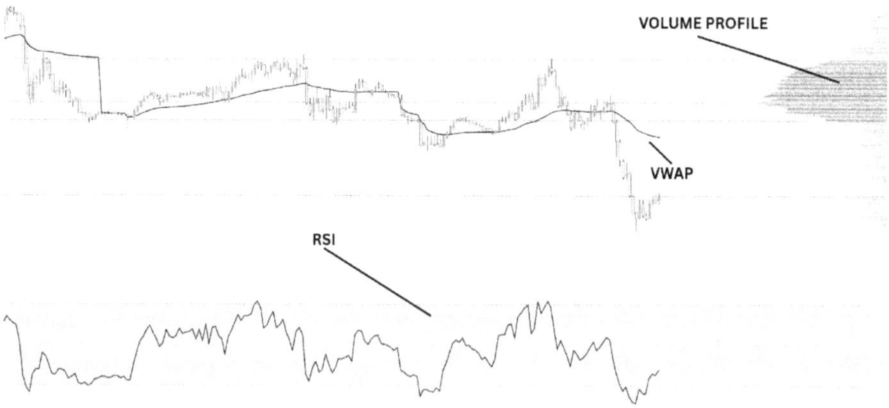

- **Reversal Play**: Bollinger Bands + Stochastic Oscillator

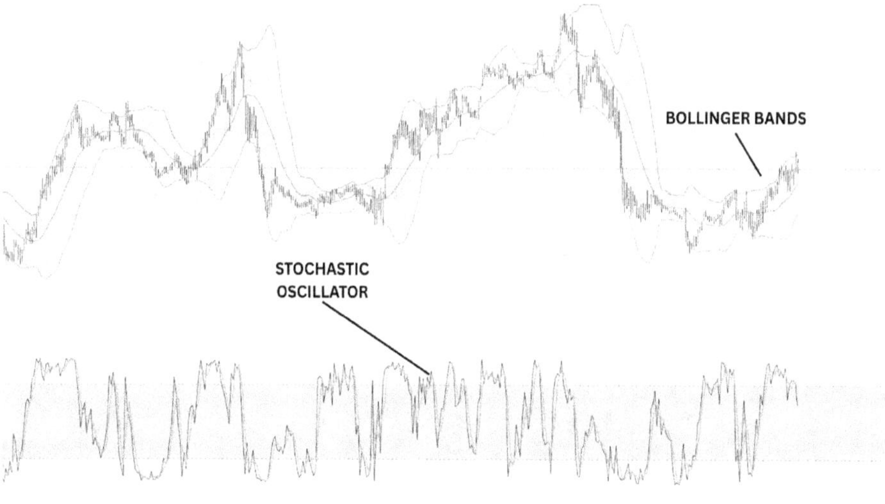

Tips for Building Your Indicator Strategy:

- Use no more than 2–3 indicators to avoid clutter.
- Backtest combinations on the futures contract you trade most.
- Trust your system and refine based on performance, not emotion.

Summary

Indicators give you a statistical and visual edge—but they don't replace market understanding. Mastering a few high-impact indicators and applying them with consistency is far more powerful than using everything at once.

Key Takeaways

✔ Moving Averages, RSI, and MACD offer trend and momentum insight—essential for all futures traders.

✔ VWAP and Volume Profile are crucial for intraday precision and institutional-level decision-making.

✔ Bollinger Bands, ATR, and Stochastic help refine entries, exits, and volatility expectations.

✔ Combine 2–3 complementary indicators for the highest signal quality and clarity.

✔ Backtest and journal every setup to refine what works best for your trading style.

Chapter 9

The Power of Routine – Developing a Daily Trading Process

Introduction

If you're serious about becoming a successful futures trader, you must develop a strong, repeatable daily trading routine. This chapter dives deep into the core structure of a professional trader's day, how to build a system that works for you, and why routine is the ultimate trading edge.

Why a Daily Routine Matters

Consistency is the foundation of profitability. A well-structured trading routine helps:

- **Eliminate emotional decision-making**
- **Keep you focused on high-probability setups**
- **Develop discipline and accountability**
- **Build a trackable performance history**
- **Allow for better optimization and refinement**

Think of your trading routine as a framework that protects your capital, keeps you in sync with the market, and helps you develop a razor-sharp edge over time.

The Three Phases of a Trading Day

A professional routine includes three distinct phases: Pre-Market, Active Trading Hours, and Post-Market Review. Each serves a purpose and contributes to your long-term consistency.

1. Pre-Market Preparation

The day starts before any trade is placed. This phase is all about mindset, market prep, and planning.

Morning Checklist:

- **Sleep & Health Check**: Ensure you're rested and focused. Fatigue leads to impulsive trades.
- **News Scan**: Use resources like Forex Factory, MarketWatch, or your broker's news feed to scan for:

    - Fed announcements
    - Earnings reports
    - Economic indicators (CPI, NFP, etc.)

- **Global Market Overview**:
    - Analyze overnight action in Asia and Europe.
    - Check S&P futures, crude oil, gold, and VIX for sentiment clues.

- **Set Key Levels**:
    - Identify support/resistance zones on higher timeframes.
    - Mark gaps, previous day's high/low, VWAP, and premarket highs/lows.

- **Review Your Plan**:
  - Write down what setups you're looking for.
  - Know your max loss for the day and position sizing.

Tools to Help:

- TradingView watchlists
- Economic calendar alerts
- Pre-market scanners

2. Active Trading Hours

This is when the markets open, and execution begins—but it's not about trading every move. It's about **waiting for your edge**.

During Market Open:

- **First 15–30 Minutes**:
  - Observe volatility without trading. Let the market establish direction.
- **Wait for Confirmation**:
  - Avoid jumping in too early. Watch for confirmation of your setup criteria.
- **Stick to Your Plan**:
  - Follow your rules for entries, exits, and stops.
- **Log Your Trades**:
  - Record details of each trade: entry, stop, target, size, rationale, and outcome.

Avoid These Mistakes:

- Overtrading due to boredom or FOMO
- Moving stops impulsively
- Revenge trading after a loss

Use the "Power Hour" Method:

Some traders focus only on high-volume times:

- **Morning Power Hour (9:30 AM – 10:30 AM ET)**
- **Lunchtime Dead Zone (11:30 AM – 1:30 PM ET):** Avoid trading unless there's major news.
- **Afternoon Power Hour (2:00 PM – 3:30 PM ET):** Often provides breakout or reversal setups.

3. Post-Market Review

This is the most overlooked phase but arguably the most important for growth.

Daily Review Checklist:

- **Trade Review**: Screenshot and annotate your trades. Ask:
    - Did I follow my plan?
    - What could I have done better?
- **Emotional Check-In**:
    - Were you calm, anxious, or overconfident?
- **Journal Key Takeaways**:
    - Log your win/loss ratio, R-multiples, and how you felt.
    - Write 1–2 improvements for tomorrow.

Weekly Performance Summary:

At the end of each week, assess:

- Total PnL
- Accuracy % (winning trades vs. total)
- Average risk/reward ratio
- Which setups worked best
- Which habits hurt you

Building the Routine That Works for You

While the routine above is a solid foundation, it must fit your lifestyle and trading style.

Personalization Tips:

- **Part-Time Traders**: Focus on one market session, like the NY open or late-day breakout windows.
- **Full-Time Traders**: Consider adding midday strategy refinement or backtesting time.
- **Swing Traders**: Review markets in the evening and prep for overnight holds.

Tools to Automate and Track:

- **Trading Journal Platforms**: Trademetria, Edgewonk, or a custom spreadsheet
- **Routine Apps**: Todoist, Notion templates for daily checklists

Developing the Trader's Mindset

A routine doesn't just keep you organized—it builds **mental toughness**.

- **Routine creates control** in a chaotic market environment.
- **Repetition creates intuition**—you'll learn to spot trades faster with less emotion.
- **Self-review creates growth**—honest journaling is where breakthroughs happen.

You'll hear successful traders say, "The edge is in the process." The daily routine is that process.

Summary

A strong, consistent trading routine gives you a clear framework for success. It eliminates emotional noise, helps you track your performance, and keeps you focused on executing high-probability trades. Over time, your routine becomes your trading edge.

Key Takeaways

✔ A structured routine builds consistency, discipline, and long-term performance.

✔ Divide your day into pre-market, active trading, and post-market review phases.

✔ Track your trades, journal your emotions, and review daily to improve.

✔ Customize your routine based on lifestyle, trading style, and market focus.

✔ Use your routine to create mental clarity and refine your edge over time.

Chapter 10

Simulated Trading – Sharpen Your Skills Without Risking Capital

Introduction

Before risking real money in the futures markets, it's essential to practice your strategy in a safe, controlled environment. Simulated trading—also known as paper trading—lets you refine your skills, test your edge, and gain confidence without financial risk. In this chapter, we'll show you how to make the most of simulation to prepare for live trading.

Why Simulated Trading is Crucial

Many new traders want to jump straight into live markets. But trading without preparation is like flying a plane without flight school. Simulated trading helps you:

- Develop discipline and consistency
- Test new strategies in real market conditions
- Build confidence by refining execution
- Track performance metrics without stress

This is the **training ground** where your trading habits are built.

Choosing a Simulator

Not all trading simulators are created equal. The best simulators mirror real market conditions with live data and full platform functionality. Here's what to look for:

Key Features to Prioritize:

- **Real-Time Market Data:** Simulators with delayed data won't give you realistic trading experiences.
- **Order Execution Options:** Your simulator should support market, limit, and stop orders like a real trading platform.
- **Charting Tools:** Ensure you have access to technical indicators, drawing tools, and multi-timeframe analysis.
- **Broker Integration:** Some platforms allow seamless transition from simulated to live trading.

Popular Simulated Trading Platforms:

- **NinjaTrader (Sim Mode)** – Full-featured with live futures data if subscribed
- **TradingView Paper Trading** – Great for strategy testing and charting practice
- **thinkorswim (PaperMoney)** – Realistic execution and full feature set
- **TradeStation Simulator** – Professional-grade, especially good for futures testing

Treat Simulated Trading Like Real Trading

The key to gaining value from simulation is taking it seriously. Here's how:

Build Good Habits:

- **Set a Starting Balance:** Match your planned live trading capital for realistic expectations.
- **Use the Same Rules:** Apply the same risk management, trade setups, and execution logic as you would live.
- **Log Your Trades:** Track your performance, analyze what worked, and identify weaknesses.
- **Limit Overtrading:** Just because it's simulated doesn't mean you should take every setup.

Track Performance:

- Win rate
- Risk-to-reward ratio
- Maximum drawdown
- Average profit per trade
- Total simulated profit/loss

These metrics give you critical insight into your edge before risking real capital.

When to Transition to Live Trading

Simulated trading is not forever. Use it to gain readiness—but move to real trading when:

- You've had at least **30–50 simulated sessions** using your full strategy
- You've shown consistent profitability and low drawdowns
- You can control emotions and avoid revenge trades or overtrading
- You've documented your rules and have a trading plan you trust

Remember, the goal is confidence through preparation.

Summary

Simulated trading is your proving ground. It gives you the chance to hone your strategy, build confidence, and eliminate costly mistakes—before they happen. Treat it seriously, track your progress, and you'll be prepared to go live with control and discipline.

Key Takeaways

✔ Simulated trading helps you develop your strategy and discipline in a no-risk environment.

✔ Choose a simulator with real-time data, full trading functionality, and realistic execution.

✔ Treat your simulation like real trading—log trades, follow your rules, and avoid overtrading.

✔ Transition to live trading only after demonstrating consistent simulated profitability and emotional control.

Chapter 11

Journaling & Tracking Results – Measure What Matters

Introduction

Great traders don't just trade—they track. If you're not journaling your trades, you're missing out on the most powerful tool for improvement. In this chapter, you'll learn how to track your performance with precision, spot patterns in your behavior, and make data-driven tweaks that lead to consistent growth.

Why Tracking Is Crucial for Success

Most beginner traders focus only on wins and losses. But pros go deeper—they analyze everything.

Benefits of Journaling and Tracking:

- **Identify winning strategies and eliminate weak ones**
- **Track emotional patterns that lead to mistakes**
- **Understand your true edge (or lack thereof)**
- **Build confidence through measured progress**

- **Turn your trading into a repeatable, scalable process**

It's impossible to improve what you don't measure. Tracking turns your trades into a feedback loop.

What to Track (Beyond Wins and Losses)

Effective journaling isn't just about numbers—it's about insights. Here's what your journal should include:

Trade Data:

- Date & time of trade
- Instrument (e.g., CL, ES, GC)
- Strategy used
- Entry & exit price
- Position size

- Stop loss and target

Performance Metrics:

- Win/loss record
- Average R-per-trade
- Max drawdown
- Win streaks/loss streaks
- Average hold time

Emotional Data:

- What were you feeling before/during/after the trade?
- Did you follow your plan?
- Were you calm or reactive?

Screenshots:

- Pre-trade setup
- Exit screenshot
- Annotations showing rationale and outcome

This combination of technical and emotional review is what makes your journal a growth engine.

The Power of Tagging & Categorization

Tagging trades helps you uncover your true strengths.

Suggested Tags:

- Strategy (breakout, pullback, trend continuation, reversal)
- Time of day (open, mid-day, close)
- Market condition (range-bound, trending, high/low volatility)
- Outcome (followed plan, stopped out early, overtraded)

Over time, you'll find surprising insights, like:

"I win 70% of my breakout trades in trending markets during the NY open—but only 30% when I trade reversals in chop."

Tools You Can Use

There are many ways to track your trades—from simple spreadsheets to premium software.

Free Options:

- Google Sheets or Excel (custom-built templates)
- Notion journal with screenshots and checklists

Paid Tools (Highly Recommended):

- **Trademetria** – Easy tracking, journaling, and performance analytics
- **Edgewonk** – In-depth analysis and psychology tracking
- **TraderSync** – Clean UI, mobile-friendly, strategy tagging
- **Journalytix** – Real-time journaling and execution review (for advanced users)

These platforms automate performance breakdowns and help you make smarter trading decisions faster.

How Often Should You Review?

Tracking isn't a "set it and forget it" system. You need to **actively review your data** to extract value.

Daily:

- Review your trades immediately after market close
- Write a 1–3 sentence reflection on what went right/wrong

Weekly:

- Review win/loss stats, screenshots, and top lessons
- Note any changes needed to your trading plan or routine

Monthly:

- Deep-dive into metrics like R-multiples, most profitable strategies, and emotional mistakes
- Adjust your strategy, size, or focus areas

The Goal: Build a Playbook

Your journal eventually becomes a **personal trading playbook**.

It tells you:

- What setups are most profitable
- What times of day you trade best
- What emotions sabotage you
- How much size you can handle with control
- What your edge truly looks like in data form

Most importantly, it gives you a **clear path to improvement.**

Summary

Every trade holds a lesson. Journaling ensures you capture those lessons and convert them into edge. With the right tracking habits, you'll build more confidence, remove destructive behaviors, and become the type of trader who wins by process—not luck.

Key Takeaways

✔ Track every trade's technical and emotional details to uncover patterns and improve performance.

✔ Use spreadsheets or professional journal tools like Trademetria, Edgewonk, or TraderSync.

✔ Tag and categorize trades by strategy, time, and market condition for deep insights.

✔ Review your journal daily, weekly, and monthly to refine your edge.

✔ Your journal is your playbook—it holds the key to consistent, scalable profits.

Chapter 12

Building Confidence and Consistency

Introduction

The futures market can be an emotional battlefield. Between the highs of big wins and the lows of drawdowns, a trader's greatest challenge is often psychological. Building lasting success in trading isn't just about mastering strategy—it's about mastering yourself. In this chapter, we'll explore how to build a resilient mindset, develop emotional discipline, and become a trader who thrives over the long run.

The Role of Mindset in Trading

Mindset is the foundation of your performance. While technical skills and strategy get you in the game, your emotional control and psychological stability determine whether you stay in it.

Traits of Consistently Profitable Traders:

- Confidence rooted in data, not ego
- Discipline to follow a proven plan
- Patience to wait for high-quality setups

- Emotional resilience during losses
- A growth mindset that embraces feedback

Building Confidence Through Preparation

Confidence is earned. It doesn't come from a lucky win—it comes from consistently doing the work behind the scenes.

Key Methods to Build Confidence:

- **Journal Every Trade:** Review what worked and what didn't.
- **Track Performance Metrics:** Let data validate your process.
- **Rehearse Your Strategy:** Backtest and simulate before trading real capital.
- **Visualize Execution:** Practice visualizing successful trades and managing adversity.

Developing Emotional Discipline

Lack of discipline is the root cause of most trading mistakes. Revenge trading, overtrading, and breaking rules all stem from emotional impulses.

Tips to Stay Disciplined:

- **Create a Trading Checklist:** Follow it before every trade.
- **Use Daily Risk Limits:** Stop trading after a certain loss threshold.
- **Trade Smaller During Stressful Days:** Preserve capital and confidence.
- **Step Away When Emotional:** Take a walk, meditate, or reset your focus.

Build Pre- and Post-Market Routines:

- **Pre-Market:** Analyze levels, check news, review your plan.

- **Post-Market:** Journal results, review setups, identify improvement areas.

Embracing the Process Over the Outcome

Long-term traders don't obsess over individual wins or losses—they focus on process. Process-driven trading removes the pressure of needing to "be right" and helps you detach from short-term outcomes.

Reframe Your Thinking:

- A losing trade executed perfectly is still a win.
- A winning trade that broke your rules is a failure.
- Consistency in behavior leads to consistency in results.

Handling Drawdowns and Slumps

Every trader faces slumps. What matters is how you handle them.

Strategies for Navigating Drawdowns:

- **Reduce Position Size:** Lower risk to reduce emotional pressure.
- **Pause and Reflect:** Stop trading to identify what's not working.
- **Focus on Execution Quality:** Forget P&L—rate yourself on discipline.
- **Talk to Other Traders:** Get perspective and support.

The Power of Reflection and Review

Consistency comes from awareness. The more you reflect on your trading behaviors, the faster you can correct and evolve.

Weekly and Monthly Reviews Should Cover:

- Best and worst trades
- Missed opportunities and why
- Rule violations
- Emotional patterns
- Areas to refine or test

Summary

Success in futures trading is as much psychological as it is technical. Confidence is built through preparation. Consistency comes from disciplined execution. And emotional resilience is what carries you through the rough patches. Master your mind—and the market will follow.

Key Takeaways

✔ Build confidence through preparation, journaling, and reviewing data—not just winning trades.

✔ Emotional discipline is a skill—use routines, risk limits, and structure to stay in control.

✔ Focus on process, not outcome, and treat each trade as a learning opportunity.

✔ Review your behavior regularly to evolve faster and trade more consistently.

Chapter 13

Advanced Execution Tactics – Trade Like a Pro Under Pressure

Introduction

Once your strategy is dialed in and your mindset is stable, your edge comes down to execution. Futures markets move fast, and the difference between a solid trade and a missed opportunity often lies in your ability to act decisively and precisely. In this chapter, we'll cover how to optimize your trade execution and react like a professional under pressure.

Why Execution Matters So Much

Even with a great strategy, poor execution can ruin a good setup. Late entries, hesitation, chasing, or slippage can all eat away at your edge. Execution bridges the gap between theory and profit.

Common Execution Errors:

- Entering too late or too early
- Letting fear or greed override your plan
- Skipping stop-loss placement
- Fumbling with order types under pressure

Mastering Order Types for Precision

Understanding how to use the right order type at the right time helps you stay in control.

Key Order Types to Master:

- **Market Orders:** Instant execution but may suffer slippage.
- **Limit Orders:** Enter at a specific price or better. Great for planned entries.
- **Stop Orders:** Trigger a market order once a price is hit (e.g., for stops or breakouts).
- **Stop-Limit Orders:** Control both price and execution—good for volatile markets.
- **Bracket Orders:** Automate your profit target and stop-loss together.

Speed vs. Control: Know When to Prioritize

Not every situation calls for lightning-fast execution. Sometimes, patience is power.

When to Prioritize Speed:

- Breakout trades in fast momentum markets
- Scalping or news-based setups
- Trading around key market opens

When to Prioritize Control:

- Fade trades (entering against momentum)
- Low-volatility range trades
- Risk-averse swing entries

Tactical Entries and Exits

Fine-tuning your entries and exits boosts your reward-to-risk ratio and reduces emotional noise.

Smart Entry Techniques:

- **Partial Fills:** Enter in pieces to average in more smoothly.
- **Confirmation Entry:** Wait for a key level break or candlestick signal.
- **Retest Entry:** Enter after the breakout when price pulls back to test support/resistance.

Smart Exit Techniques:

- **Scaling Out:** Lock in profits as the trade moves in your favor.
- **Trailing Stop:** Let winners run while protecting your downside.
- **Time-Based Exits:** Close the trade if your thesis isn't playing out within a set time.

Execution Under Pressure

In high-volatility situations, your ability to stay calm and react fast matters most.

How to Stay Composed:

- **Predefine Scenarios:** Map out your possible actions before you trade.
- **Use Hotkeys or Macros:** Faster execution with fewer clicks.
- **Practice in Replay Mode:** Simulate pressure to build confidence.
- **Use the DOM (Depth of Market):** For precise entries and exits, especially in scalping.

"Pros don't hesitate—they prepare."

Advanced Execution Tools

If your platform supports it, these tools can give you an edge in precision.

Tools to Explore:

- **One-Cancels-Other (OCO):** Automate your target/stop logic.
- **Auto-Breakeven Scripts:** Move your stop to breakeven after a set profit.
- **Dynamic Scaling Tools:** Adjust position size live based on trade progress.
- **Volume Profile or Order Flow Tools:** Add micro-structure awareness to execution.

Summary

Strong execution is what turns potential profits into real ones. It's where preparation, mindset, and tools meet under real-time pressure. The pros separate themselves with their ability to remain sharp, disciplined, and fluid when it counts.

Key Takeaways

✔ Master your order types and use the right one for the right market condition.

✔ Use precision tactics like retest entries, bracket orders, and scaling exits to manage risk and boost returns.

✔ In fast markets, preplanning and platform mastery are your greatest allies.

✔ Advanced tools like DOM, hotkeys, and auto-bracket scripts help you stay fast and focused.

Chapter 14

Volume Analysis & Order Flow – Decode the Market's Intentions

Introduction

In futures trading, volume and order flow give you direct insight into the actions of market participants. Price can be misleading without context, but when you combine it with volume and the dynamics of order flow, you gain a clearer understanding of **who is in control**, **where key activity is occurring**, and **when the market may be poised to move**. This chapter will guide you through the core concepts of volume and order flow, the tools you need to analyze them, and how to incorporate them into your futures trading strategy.

Understanding Volume in Futures Trading

Volume represents the total number of contracts traded in a given time frame. Unlike stocks, where volume is tied to shares, futures volume reflects actual contract transactions. This makes it an incredibly pure form of market participation data.

Why Volume Matters:

- **Confirms Price Action:** Rising prices with rising volume suggest strength; rising prices with falling volume suggest weakness.

- **Identifies Reversals:** Volume spikes can signal exhaustion or climactic turning points.
- **Validates Breakouts:** High volume breakouts are more reliable than low volume ones.

Types of Volume to Watch:

- **Tick Volume:** Measures the number of price changes (often used when actual volume data is not available).
- **Actual Volume:** Total contracts traded—most accurate for futures.
- **Relative Volume (RVOL):** Compares current volume to an average—used to gauge unusual activity.

Volume Profile – The Market's Footprint

Volume Profile is a powerful visualization tool that shows how much volume has traded at each price level over a specific time period. It paints a clear picture of **value zones**, **support/resistance**, and **market acceptance or rejection**.

Key Volume Profile Concepts:

- **Point of Control (POC):** The price level with the highest volume.
- **Value Area (VA):** The range where 70% of trading occurred.
- **High Volume Node (HVN):** Areas of consolidation or acceptance.
- **Low Volume Node (LVN):** Areas of rejection—great zones for entries or exits.

Use Cases:

- **Identify support/resistance levels** based on prior volume concentration.
- **Recognize areas of accumulation/distribution.**
- **Set entries and exits** around volume-based zones.

Order Flow Analysis – Seeing the Invisible

Order flow analysis involves observing the actual buying and selling activity at the bid and ask. This level of transparency is made possible through tools like the **Depth of Market (DOM)** and **footprint charts**.

Key Tools:

- **Footprint Charts:** Display real-time executed volume at each price level, typically showing:
    - **Bid x Ask volume**

    - **Delta (Buy volume – Sell volume)**
    - **Cumulative Delta**
- **Depth of Market (DOM):** Shows current limit orders at each price level.
    - Highlights **liquidity zones**, **spoofing**, and **absorbing orders.**

Why Order Flow Matters:

- Reveals **real-time market intent**.
- Exposes **aggressive buyers/sellers** entering the market.
- Helps you understand **trapped traders** and **potential squeezes**.

Key Indicators for Volume and Order Flow

Here are some of the most powerful indicators used by professional futures traders to assess volume and flow dynamics:

1. Volume Weighted Average Price (VWAP)

- Acts as an intraday mean reversion point.
- Institutions often buy below and sell above VWAP.
- Supports scalping and swing trading entries.

2. Cumulative Delta

- Measures the net difference between aggressive buyers and sellers.
- **Positive divergence:** Buyers stepping in despite falling prices.

- **Negative divergence:** Sellers dominating in rising prices.

3. Market Delta / Footprint Tools

- Analyze whether trades are lifting the ask or hitting the bid.
- Spot imbalance or exhaustion in moves.

4. On-Balance Volume (OBV)

- Tracks cumulative volume based on price direction.
- Useful for identifying breakouts and divergences.

5. Volume Oscillator

- Measures the difference between short and long-term volume averages.
- Great for identifying momentum in volume surges.

6. Delta Divergence Zones

- Areas where cumulative delta and price diverge, signaling possible turning points.

7. Volume Clusters and Imbalances

- Analyze zones of stacked buying/selling pressure to anticipate movement.

Real-World Application

Let's walk through a scenario using volume and order flow in oil futures (CL):

1. **Volume Profile:** The POC is sitting at $83.45 on the daily chart. This is a key magnet level.

2. **Footprint Chart:** Shows large buy imbalances at $82.90 and $83.00, indicating aggressive buyers.

3. **Cumulative Delta:** Trending up while price remains rangebound—hidden accumulation.

4. **Trade Plan:** Go long on a dip to $82.85 with a target at $83.70 (just above the POC).

This approach gives you a **clear framework backed by real market activity**, not just chart patterns or lagging indicators.

Building a Volume & Order Flow-Based Strategy

You can build an entire system around volume and flow, or you can integrate it into your existing strategy for confirmation.

Tips:

- Always combine volume with **context** (trend, structure, timeframe).
- Use order flow to **fine-tune entries and exits.**
- Watch for **fakeouts** in low volume areas.
- Practice reading **footprint and DOM data** on replay to get comfortable.

Summary

Price is only half the story—volume and order flow reveal the true intent behind every candle. By learning to read this data, you'll gain a trader's intuition that goes far beyond indicators and chart patterns. Futures traders who master volume and flow often develop a true **edge that stands the test of time**.

Key Takeaways

✔ Volume confirms or contradicts price action—use it to assess trend strength and breakout reliability.

✔ Volume Profile helps identify key value zones and high-probability support/resistance levels.

✔ Order flow tools like footprint charts and the DOM show you real-time buying and selling aggression.

✔ Cumulative delta, VWAP, and volume imbalances are essential tools for tracking market sentiment.

✔ Integrating volume and order flow improves precision, enhances timing, and builds confidence in your trades.

Chapter 15

Multi-Timeframe Analysis – Improve Your Trade Accuracy

Introduction

Many new traders get stuck making decisions based on a single chart. They focus too closely on short-term signals and miss the bigger picture. Multi-timeframe analysis (MTFA) helps you align your entries and exits with broader market context. By evaluating different timeframes—such as daily, hourly, and intraday—you gain better accuracy, improved timing, and increased confidence in your trades.

In this chapter, we'll break down how to use multiple timeframes to enhance your futures trading performance, avoid false signals, and capture more precise opportunities.

Why Multi-Timeframe Analysis Matters

Markets operate in layers. Price action on a 1-minute chart may seem chaotic, but that movement could be just noise within a larger trend unfolding on a 4-hour chart.

Key Benefits of MTFA:

- **Confirms Trend Direction:** Trade with the dominant trend on higher timeframes.

- **Filters Low-Quality Setups:** Avoid going against key levels or structure.

- **Improves Timing:** Use smaller timeframes for refined entries and exits.

The Three-Frame Structure

Traders often use a “top-down” approach with three core timeframes:

1. Higher Timeframe (HTF) – Market Context

- Example: Daily or 4-hour chart.

- **Purpose:** Defines overall trend and structure (support, resistance, breakouts).

- Ask: *Are we in an uptrend, downtrend, or consolidation?*

2. Trading Timeframe (TF) – Setup

- Example: 1-hour or 15-minute chart.

- **Purpose:** Identifies actionable setups and chart patterns.
- Ask: *Is there a flag, breakout, or reversal structure forming?*

3. Entry Timeframe (ETF) – Precision

- Example: 5-minute or 1-minute chart.
- **Purpose:** Fine-tunes your entry and stop-loss based on price behavior.
- Ask: *Is there a strong candle close, volume confirmation, or order flow signal?*

How to Build a Multi-Timeframe Routine

Here's a simple step-by-step framework to apply MTFA in your daily trading routine:

Step 1: Analyze the Higher Timeframe

- Mark key support/resistance zones.
- Identify market structure (trend, ranges, breakouts).
- Note high volume nodes or previous day highs/lows.

Step 2: Spot Setups on the Trading Timeframe

- Look for clean chart patterns or price consolidations.
- Use indicators like VWAP, moving averages, or RSI to confirm bias.
- Watch for pullbacks, retests, or compression patterns near HTF levels.

Step 3: Execute on the Entry Timeframe

- Wait for confirmation with candles, volume, or footprint signals.
- Enter at areas of confluence—HTF structure + TF setup + ETF trigger.
- Keep stops tight below ETF structure and manage risk based on HTF zones.

Example: Multi-Timeframe Trade in Gold Futures (GC)

1. **Daily Chart (HTF):** Bullish trend, price is pulling back to a rising 20 EMA and previous breakout level at $2,050.
2. **15-Min Chart (TF):** Double bottom forming at $2,050 with decreasing volume on the second dip.
3. **1-Min Chart (ETF):** Bullish engulfing candle with aggressive delta and bid absorption.

Trade Plan: Long entry at $2,052, stop at $2,047, target $2,065.

Multi-Timeframe Indicator Strategies

Many traders use the same indicators across different timeframes. Here are a few combinations that work well:

Moving Averages

- 200 EMA on HTF defines trend bias.
- 50 EMA on TF signals pullback opportunities.
- 9/21 EMAs on ETF provide dynamic entry zones.

RSI / Momentum

- Overbought/oversold signals on HTF suggest broader market sentiment.
- Divergences on TF + ETF give entry confirmation.

VWAP

- HTF VWAP acts as a magnet or barrier.
- Use VWAP reclaims or rejections on TF/ETF to time entries.

Avoid These Common MTFA Mistakes

Trading Against the Higher Timeframe

- If the daily is bearish, avoid long setups unless there's a clear reversal signal.

Getting Stuck on Lower Timeframes

- The 1-minute chart may look bullish, but the 4-hour could be breaking down. Always zoom out.

Overcomplicating

- Stick to 2–3 timeframes. Too many creates confusion and analysis paralysis.

Summary

Multi-timeframe analysis gives you an edge that many retail traders ignore. By combining broader context with refined entries, you'll make more consistent and confident trading decisions. It's like switching from tunnel vision to a wide-angle lens—your trades become more intentional, aligned, and precise.

Key Takeaways

✔ Use a top-down approach—analyze trend and structure on higher timeframes, find setups on trading timeframes, and time entries on lower timeframes.

✔ Combine price action with volume, indicators, and order flow across all timeframes.

✔ Avoid trading against dominant higher-timeframe trends unless a clear reversal setup forms.

✔ MTFA increases win rates, improves trade timing, and enhances overall trade quality.

Chapter 16

Futures Trading Psychology – Build Discipline, Focus, and Resilience

Introduction

Technical skill is only half the battle in futures trading. Your mindset, emotional control, and mental resilience often determine whether you stay consistent—or blow up your account. In fast-paced futures markets, psychological discipline is critical for long-term success.

This chapter explores how to build emotional resilience, stick to your plan, and trade with a focused, professional mindset.

Why Trading Psychology Is Everything

You can have the best strategy in the world, but without discipline, it won't matter. The futures market is unforgiving to traders who overtrade, revenge trade, or panic under pressure.

Psychological Challenges Futures Traders Face:

- Fear of missing out (FOMO)
- Overconfidence after a winning streak
- Impulsive revenge trading after a loss

- Doubting your plan in high volatility
- Chasing trades or ignoring your stop-loss

The Trader's Emotional Cycle

Every trader experiences a repeating cycle of emotions. The goal is to become aware of these phases—and act with logic rather than emotion.

Common Phases:

1. **Euphoria:** After a winning streak, you feel invincible and start risking more.
2. **Anxiety:** A few losses make you second-guess setups you used to trust.
3. **Fear:** You hesitate on valid trades, afraid to pull the trigger.
4. **Desperation:** You break your rules, double your size, and try to "win it all back."

5. **Acceptance:** You reset, return to discipline, and trade your plan.

How to Build Discipline and Mental Toughness

1. Create and Follow a Rules-Based System

- Have strict criteria for when you enter, size up, and exit.
- Automate decisions where possible (via alerts or limit orders).

2. Use a Pre-Trade Checklist

- Check trend alignment, risk/reward, market news, and mental state before entering.

3. Track Your Emotions in a Trade Journal

- Write down your mindset before and after trades to identify patterns.

- Example: *"Took this trade out of boredom"* → *Fix: Only trade your A+ setups.*

4. Practice Mental Rehearsal

- Visualize yourself managing trades with calm, even in high volatility.
- This improves confidence and helps program consistency.

5. Learn to Walk Away

- One of the most powerful skills: knowing when *not* to trade.
- If you feel angry, tilted, or emotionally charged—step away.

The Role of Self-Awareness

Successful traders know their triggers.

Ask yourself:

- Do I get emotional after a loss?
- Do I overtrade when I'm bored or feeling down?
- Do I stick to my stop-loss or move it out of fear?

Write down your habits. Track your progress. Hold yourself accountable.

Practical Daily Habits for Strong Psychology

- **Morning routine:** Review your plan and do a quick meditation or mindset exercise.
- **Journal post-trade:** What did you do well? What needs work?
- **Set max trades per day:** Avoid overtrading and mental fatigue.
- **Take breaks:** Step away from the screen to reset your focus.

Reframing Losses

Losses are part of the game. Instead of seeing them as failures, reframe them as feedback.

Ask:

- Did I follow my rules?
- Was this trade within my strategy?
- What can I improve next time?

Trading is a performance skill—like sports or music. Mistakes aren't personal—they're learning tools.

Mental Edge in Futures Trading

The futures market demands more mental stamina than most markets. You're dealing with leverage, speed, and volatility. To thrive, you need:

- Patience to wait for high-probability setups.
- Courage to pull the trigger with confidence.
- Humility to accept losses and stay grounded.
- Grit to keep going after setbacks.

Summary

You are your own biggest asset—and your biggest risk. Technical tools help you trade, but psychology determines whether you can stay consistent. The traders who win long-term are those who develop iron discipline, emotional control, and a mindset focused on process over outcome.

Key Takeaways

✔ Trading psychology is just as important as technical skill—especially in fast-moving futures markets.

✔ Develop self-awareness, emotional discipline, and a consistent mindset to maintain peak performance.

✔ Use tools like trade journaling, mental rehearsal, and daily checklists to keep your psychology in check.

✔ Treat losses as feedback and focus on long-term consistency, not short-term outcomes.

Chapter 17

Developing Your Signature Trading Style – Aligning Strategy With Personality

Introduction

Every successful futures trader eventually develops their own trading identity—one that aligns with their strengths, personality, and lifestyle. Instead of copying someone else's method, the most consistent traders evolve a style that feels natural and repeatable.

In this chapter, you'll learn how to refine your trading approach based on your unique traits and preferences, and how to turn that approach into a consistent edge.

Why Your Trading Style Matters

Trying to follow someone else's strategy word for word can lead to frustration. What works for one trader may not fit your risk tolerance, psychology, or schedule. Your trading style should feel intuitive and sustainable—not forced.

Benefits of a Personalized Trading Style:

- Greater emotional control
- Better execution under pressure
- Easier journaling and performance review

- Stronger confidence and consistency

Assessing Your Trader Profile

Before you can define your style, you need to understand your tendencies.

Key Questions to Ask:

- **How much screen time do I realistically have per day?**
- **Do I prefer quick trades or longer holds?**
- **How well do I handle risk and volatility?**
- **Do I thrive in fast action or structured environments?**
- **Do I prefer rule-based or discretionary trading?**

Your answers help define the building blocks of your trading identity.

Trading Styles in Futures

There's no "one-size-fits-all." Here are the most common styles among futures traders:

1. Scalper

- **Timeframe:** Seconds to a few minutes
- **Traits:** Fast decision-making, loves volatility
- **Tools:** DOM, footprint charts, tick charts
- **Markets:** Crude oil (CL), E-mini S&P (ES)

2. Day Trader

- **Timeframe:** In and out within the same session
- **Traits:** Enjoys clean structure, medium volatility
- **Tools:** 1–15 min charts, volume profile, VWAP
- **Markets:** Gold (GC), Nasdaq (NQ), ES

3. Swing Trader

- **Timeframe:** Hold trades from overnight to several days
- **Traits:** Patient, prefers less screen time
- **Tools:** 1-hour, 4-hour, and daily charts
- **Markets:** Index futures, bonds, commodities

4. Position Trader

- **Timeframe:** Weeks to months
- **Traits:** Long-term thinker, unaffected by noise
- **Tools:** Daily and weekly charts, macro trends
- **Markets:** Commodity and currency futures

Mixing Strategies Based on Market Conditions

Many traders adapt between styles based on volatility and clarity in the markets.

- **Choppy markets:** Favor scalping and fade setups
- **Trending markets:** Use breakout or swing strategies
- **News events:** Trade volatility carefully or stay flat

Flexibility helps you survive and thrive across different conditions.

Building Around Your Strengths

Every trader has a few natural strengths—those are your superpowers. Build your strategy around them.

Strength-Based Examples:

- If you're analytical → Structure your trades with rule-based entry and exit.

- If you're intuitive → Use discretionary setups with volume and price action cues.
- If you're emotional → Stick to automated entries and tight risk management.

Play to your edge. Don't fight your nature.

Customizing Risk & Money Management

Your personal risk tolerance is critical. Just because someone else trades 10 contracts doesn't mean you should.

- **Test sizing slowly:** Increase only when consistency is proven.
- **Set realistic goals:** Focus on process, not daily P&L.
- **Know your breaking point:** Avoid emotional triggers and revenge trading.

Journaling to Discover Your Ideal Style

Trade journaling reveals patterns in your performance and mindset.

Track:

- Which trades feel most natural?
- Which setups cause hesitation or regret?
- When are you most focused and decisive?

Your journal is a goldmine for refining your personal style.

Finalizing Your Signature Strategy

Once you've tested enough, lock in your "A+ setup."

Your Signature Strategy Should Include:

- A clear setup with defined entry/exit rules
- Preferred markets and timeframes
- Position sizing model
- Risk management protocol
- Mental prep routine

Your strategy becomes your trading identity—the blueprint you return to again and again.

Summary

The most successful traders aren't the ones with the fanciest tools—they're the ones who truly know themselves. When you tailor your trading strategy to your personality, the market becomes a lot less stressful and a lot more profitable.

Key Takeaways

✔ Your trading strategy should align with your strengths, schedule, and risk tolerance.

✔ Define your trading style—scalping, day trading, swing trading, or position trading.

✔ Use trade journaling to discover your natural edge and performance trends.

✔ Your signature strategy should be structured, tested, and aligned with your personality.

Chapter 18

The Power of Journaling and Review – Build a System That Learns With You

Introduction

Consistent profitability in futures trading isn't just about finding good setups—it's about learning from your past. The most successful traders in the world treat journaling and trade reviews as essential components of their edge.

In this chapter, you'll learn how to set up a journaling process that not only tracks your trades but evolves your strategy over time. Think of it as building a feedback loop between your execution and improvement.

Why Journaling Matters in Futures Trading

Every trade you take holds valuable data—whether it wins or loses. When you log your trades consistently, patterns emerge. You start to see which setups work best, which times of day are strongest, and what emotions might be holding you back.

Benefits of Journaling:

- Clarifies what's working and what's not

- Helps reduce emotional and impulsive trades
- Builds self-awareness around execution and mindset
- Creates a personal database for refining your edge

What to Record in a Trading Journal

To get the most value, you need to go beyond just logging entries and exits. Include both technical and emotional data.

Trade Data to Track:

- Instrument traded (e.g., CL, ES, GC)
- Entry price and exit price
- Stop loss and target
- Position size and result (win/loss)
- Time and date of trade
- Timeframe used (1-min, 5-min, 15-min, etc.)

- Setup type (e.g., VWAP bounce, trend continuation)
- Reason for taking the trade (what was the edge?)

Emotional & Execution Notes:

- How confident were you in the setup?
- Did you follow your rules?
- Any hesitation or second-guessing?
- How did you feel before/during/after the trade?

Tools for Journaling

You can keep it simple or go advanced, depending on your preference.

Basic Tools:

- Spreadsheet (Excel, Google Sheets)

- Notion or OneNote
- Physical notebook

Advanced Tools:

- Trade Journal software (e.g., TraderSync, Edgewonk, Tradervue)
- Broker-integrated journal exports
- Screen recording tools (OBS Studio, Loom) to review chart action

Reviewing Your Journal

Journaling is only powerful when you review it. Make it a weekly habit.

What to Look For in Reviews:

- Which setups are the most profitable?
- Are you sticking to your rules?
- Do you overtrade during specific hours?
- Are certain emotions tied to poor performance?

Use this data to make tactical changes: eliminate weak setups, adjust size, or rework risk protocols.

Creating a Playbook of Winning Setups

Once you've logged and reviewed dozens of trades, start organizing your best trades into a *playbook.*

Each Play Should Include:

- Setup name and detailed description
- Screenshot of the chart with annotations
- Entry/exit examples
- Ideal market conditions
- Emotional mindset to look for (e.g., confidence, calmness)

Tracking Performance Over Time

Don’t just look at individual trades—track your *overall* growth.

Track Metrics Like:

- Win rate (%)
- Average R/R (risk-to-reward)
- Monthly profit/loss
- Max drawdown
- Consistency over 20–50 trades

Watching your metrics improve builds massive confidence and proves your strategy’s edge.

The Growth Loop: Journal → Review → Adjust

Here's how elite traders improve continuously:

1. **Trade**
2. **Journal the trade**
3. **Review your journal weekly**
4. **Adjust your plan or mindset**
5. **Repeat**

This process compounds. Over time, small tweaks create massive breakthroughs.

Summary

Every trade teaches something—if you're paying attention. Journaling is your mirror. It shows you not only what your strategy is doing but what *you* are doing. And when you combine that awareness with discipline and review, your performance will compound faster than you ever expected.

Key Takeaways

✔ Journaling helps you turn every trade—win or lose—into actionable feedback.

✔ Record both technical and emotional data to improve your discipline and edge.

✔ Build a personal playbook of high-quality, repeatable setups.

✔ Review your trades weekly and track performance metrics to evolve over time.

Chapter 19

Handling Losing Streaks – Staying Confident Through the Storm

Introduction

Every trader, no matter how skilled, experiences losing streaks. They're a natural part of the trading journey—but how you handle them determines whether you come out stronger or spiral into a cycle of self-doubt and bad decisions. This chapter is about learning to *weather the storm*, stay mentally sharp, and come back more refined and focused than ever.

Understanding Losing Streaks

Losing streaks are often the result of multiple intertwined factors:

1. Market Conditions

Markets go through phases—trending, ranging, volatile, or flat. Your strategy may perform well in one condition and struggle in another. If your system isn't aligned with the current environment, even your best setups can fail.

2. Overtrading & Revenge Trading

After a loss, many traders feel the urge to immediately "win it back." This leads to impulsive trades that are emotionally driven, not data-backed.

3. Fatigue & Burnout

Mental exhaustion and lack of sleep drastically reduce decision-making ability. Many losing streaks can be traced to cognitive fatigue rather than poor strategy.

4. Strategy Drift

Traders start improvising or deviating from their plan when they feel uncertain. One or two “off-script” trades can quickly lead to several losses in a row.

The Emotional Toll of Losing Streaks

Losing streaks hit your confidence hard. You may start questioning:

- Your edge
- Your ability to trade
- Whether trading is for you at all

This emotional spiral can amplify poor decisions. It's critical to pause and reflect—*not react*.

Common Mental Patterns During a Losing Streak:

- **Confirmation Bias:** Only seeing evidence that supports your negative emotions.
- **Over-Correction:** Constantly tweaking your strategy without enough data.
- **Self-Blame or External Blame:** Either "I'm terrible" or "The market is rigged"—both are disempowering.

- **Fear to Re-Enter:** Avoiding the market out of fear, missing high-quality setups when the streak ends.

Tactical Steps to Break the Losing Streak

Here's a structured process to reset and recover your edge:

1. Stop Trading Temporarily

Take a day or two off. Clear your mind. You wouldn't keep driving if your brakes were failing—same logic applies here.

2. Review Your Trade Journal

Dive deep into your journal. Are you following your plan? Is your setup still valid in this market condition? Identify the pattern in your recent losses.

3. Simplify Your Strategy

Strip it back to your *highest probability* setups only. Stop trading marginal or experimental trades during recovery periods.

4. Reduce Position Size

Lower your size to ease emotional pressure. This reduces the stakes and allows you to focus on execution rather than outcome.

5. Return to Sim Trading

Run through the same strategy on a simulator for a few days. This helps rebuild trust in your process without financial risk.

6. Reset Expectations

Your goal isn't to "make back the losses fast"—it's to return to *discipline and consistency.* Profits will follow when your edge returns.

Mindset Tools for Staying Strong

To navigate losing streaks, your mindset needs to be bulletproof.

Affirmation Practice

Daily affirmations may sound cheesy—but they help rewire negative internal dialogue. Examples:

- *"My edge plays out over time."*
- *"Losses are part of the process."*
- *"I follow my plan without emotion."*

Visualization

Mentally rehearse placing trades with confidence and sticking to your rules. This conditions your brain to act from discipline instead of fear.

Emotional Journaling

Log not just the *what* of your trades, but the *why*. Write how you felt before, during, and after each trade. You'll quickly see if fear or hope is driving your behavior.

Exercise & Nutrition

Fuel your mind by taking care of your body. Walking, lifting weights, and eating clean all help balance your mental state and focus.

Signs That You're Back on Track

You'll know you're breaking out of the losing streak when:

- You're placing trades without hesitation or fear.
- Your setups are executed based on rules, not gut feel.
- Your wins and losses look like your backtested results.
- You feel calm—win or lose.

Advanced Recovery Tactics

1. Peer Review

Ask a fellow trader to audit your trades. A fresh set of eyes can reveal blind spots and confirm whether you're staying true to your edge.

2. Strategy Audit

Backtest your recent strategy across current market conditions. If it's not producing results even historically, you may need to tweak or sideline it temporarily.

3. Volatility Adjustment

Markets may have increased or decreased volatility. If your stops are too tight or targets too far, adjust them to fit the environment.

4. Account Segmentation

Create a "recovery mode" sub-account with strict rules and limited capital. This protects your main balance while giving you room to recalibrate.

Summary

Losing streaks are inevitable. But instead of seeing them as failure, treat them as a signal—a message that it's time to slow down, realign, and sharpen your edge.

Traders who succeed long term aren't those who avoid losses, but those who recover from them with focus, humility, and strength.

Key Takeaways

✔ Losing streaks happen to everyone—it's how you respond that matters.

✔ Step back, assess your trades, and return only when mentally and technically reset.

✔ Use mental tools like affirmations, journaling, and visualization to rebuild confidence.

✔ Focus on high-probability setups with reduced risk until consistency returns.

✔ Long-term success in futures trading comes from discipline, not from chasing lost profits.

Chapter 20

Navigating Economic Events – Mastering News-Based Futures Trading

Introduction

In the fast-paced world of futures trading, economic events play a significant role in shaping market movements. From central bank meetings to employment reports and geopolitical events, news can drastically impact prices, creating both opportunities and risks for traders. This chapter will cover how to navigate and trade around these economic events with confidence and precision.

Understanding the Impact of Economic Events

Economic events can cause sharp price fluctuations in the futures markets. Some of these events have scheduled releases, while others may occur unpredictably. Understanding the nature of these events and how they influence price action is essential for any futures trader.

Types of Economic Events:

- **Scheduled Economic Reports**: These include reports like GDP growth, unemployment numbers, consumer price index (CPI), and more. They tend to have a predictable impact on the markets, as traders can anticipate the release dates and adjust their strategies accordingly.

- **Central Bank Announcements**: Central banks like the Federal Reserve (Fed) in the U.S., the European Central Bank (ECB), and the Bank of Japan (BOJ) influence markets significantly. Interest rate decisions, monetary policy statements, and press conferences can drive significant volatility in markets.

- **Geopolitical Events**: Unexpected events like wars, elections, or political instability can cause market disruptions. While these events are unpredictable, they often lead to heightened market volatility.

- **Corporate Earnings Reports**: For index futures, particularly, the release of earnings reports by major companies can have a ripple effect on the overall market, affecting investor sentiment and market direction.

Preparing for News-Driven Volatility

Futures markets often exhibit sharp price movements ahead of or immediately following major economic announcements. Traders who are unprepared can find themselves caught in volatile moves, leading to large drawdowns or missed opportunities. To effectively trade news-driven volatility, it is important to:

1. Know the Key Economic Reports

Some economic reports are more influential than others. For example:

- **Non-Farm Payrolls (NFP)**: The U.S. job report, released on the first Friday of every month, often causes significant movement in the E-mini S&P 500 futures (ES), crude oil futures (CL), and other major futures.

- **Federal Reserve Meetings**: Interest rate decisions and statements by the Federal Reserve can influence major currency pairs, as well as commodity and index futures.

- **GDP Reports**: These can indicate the overall health of an economy and may trigger large price swings in futures markets.

2. Plan Ahead with a News Calendar

Economic news calendars are invaluable tools for futures traders. Websites like **Investing.com** or **Forex Factory** offer free economic calendars that list the dates and times for major economic events. By using these calendars, you can identify when reports or announcements are coming up and adjust your trading plan accordingly.

Tip: It's important to factor in the expected volatility surrounding these events. As a general rule, the closer the event is to release, the more the market will start to price in potential outcomes.

3. Anticipate the Market Reaction

While traders can anticipate the occurrence of news events, predicting how the market will react can be more challenging. Markets tend to move based on expectations versus the actual outcome of economic data. For instance, if the market expects strong employment data, and the report is weaker than anticipated, the market may react negatively.

Tip: Pay attention to consensus forecasts, which are available on financial websites. Compare these expectations to past trends and historical data to gauge potential market reactions. This helps you prepare for unexpected outcomes.

Managing Risk During High Volatility

Economic news events often cause sharp price movements in a short amount of time, leading to increased volatility. This can be a double-edged sword for traders, as it presents both high-profit potential and significant risk.

1. Use Smaller Position Sizes

One way to manage risk during news events is by reducing position sizes. Since volatility can be unpredictable, smaller position sizes can help mitigate the risk of large losses while still giving you the opportunity to capture profits from price movement.

2. Set Wider Stop-Loss Orders

During periods of heightened volatility, it's a good idea to widen your stop-loss orders. Standard stop-loss orders may get hit too easily during erratic market movements. Allowing for some wiggle room can help you avoid being prematurely stopped out.

3. Trade Only Major Economic Events

If you are new to trading news events, it's best to start with the major economic releases like the Non-Farm Payrolls (NFP) or Federal Reserve meetings. These events are more likely to lead to predictable and significant price moves, making them easier to trade.

Summary

By understanding the impact of economic events and preparing for market volatility, you can become a more confident and strategic trader. Whether you choose to trade before or after news releases, proper research, preparation, and risk management will help you navigate the fast-moving world of news-based futures trading.

Key Takeaways

✔ Economic events such as central bank decisions, GDP reports, and geopolitical events can drastically impact futures markets.

✔ Use economic calendars to prepare for scheduled events and anticipate market reactions.

✔ Choose to trade pre-news, post-news, or a combination of both, based on your strategy and risk tolerance.

✔ Use smaller position sizes and wider stop-loss orders to manage risk during volatile news releases.

Chapter 21

Understanding Market Sentiment – Leveraging Crowd Psychology in Futures Trading

Introduction

Market sentiment is a critical aspect of successful futures trading, as it reflects the collective emotions and psychology of market participants. While technical analysis and chart patterns provide insight into price movements, understanding market sentiment can give you a significant edge in predicting price direction. In this chapter, we'll delve into the concept of market sentiment, how to assess it, and ways to leverage crowd psychology to enhance your trading decisions.

The Role of Market Sentiment in Futures Trading

Market sentiment represents the general mood of traders and investors regarding a particular asset or market. It can be categorized as either **bullish** (optimistic) or **bearish** (pessimistic), but it also encompasses more nuanced emotions such as fear, greed, uncertainty, and confidence. Futures markets are particularly sensitive to sentiment, as they are driven by both macroeconomic factors and market psychology.

Why Market Sentiment Matters:

- **Price Movements:** Sentiment plays a key role in driving price trends. Understanding the collective mood helps predict potential reversals or continuations in the market.

- **Market Psychology:** Recognizing when market sentiment is overly optimistic or overly pessimistic can signal impending corrections, bubbles, or irrational exuberance.

- **Behavioral Biases:** Human psychology often leads to predictable market behavior, such as herd mentality and panic selling. Understanding these patterns helps in identifying price extremes.

Tools for Analyzing Market Sentiment

While sentiment can be difficult to quantify, several tools and techniques can help traders gauge the mood of the market. These tools provide insights into the psychological state of market participants and help predict potential shifts in market behavior.

1. The COT Report (Commitments of Traders)

The **COT Report** is released weekly by the Commodity Futures Trading Commission (CFTC) and shows the positioning of large institutional traders versus retail traders. It provides a snapshot of market sentiment, offering insights into whether big players are bullish or bearish on a specific futures contract.

- **How to Use It:** Look for extreme positioning in the market. When large institutions are highly bullish or bearish, the market could be near a turning point. Conversely, if retail traders are overly optimistic or pessimistic, it could indicate that the market is overextended.

2. Volatility Indicators

Volatility indicators like the **VIX (Volatility Index)** are crucial for assessing market sentiment, particularly during periods of uncertainty. The VIX tracks the implied volatility of options on the S&P 500, which reflects how fearful or confident investors are.

- **How to Use It:** A rising VIX typically signals increased fear and uncertainty, while a falling VIX indicates a more optimistic sentiment. Traders can use the VIX to anticipate market reversals, as extreme readings often precede major price corrections.

3. Social Media & News Sentiment Analysis

In the digital age, sentiment is increasingly shaped by the vast amount of information shared on social media and news platforms. Analyzing the tone of discussions on platforms like Twitter, Reddit, and financial news websites can provide insights into retail sentiment.

- **How to Use It:** Tools like **Sentiment Analysis Software** can help process social media data to gauge the overall sentiment around a particular asset. Positive buzz on social media may signal rising optimism, while widespread negativity may indicate bearish sentiment.

4. Market Breadth Indicators

Market breadth indicators track the participation of stocks or contracts in a rally or decline. These indicators, such as the **Advance-Decline Line**, can help assess whether a trend is supported by broad market participation or if it's driven by a narrow group of assets.

- **How to Use It:** A strong bullish trend with healthy breadth suggests that the sentiment is strong and sustainable. On the other hand, a rally fueled by a few stocks may signal an unsustainable, sentiment-driven move that could reverse soon.

Identifying Sentiment Extremes

One of the most powerful ways to use market sentiment is by identifying sentiment extremes. When the market is overly optimistic or pessimistic, it often signals an opportunity for a market reversal.

1. Contrarian Indicators

Contrarian indicators rely on the idea that when the majority of participants are extremely bullish or bearish, the market may be nearing an extreme. These indicators can be applied to various markets, including futures.

- **How to Use It:** Watch for extreme bullishness when everyone is calling for higher prices or extreme bearishness when the consensus is doom and gloom. This can indicate a potential reversal, as prices often overshoot before correcting.

2. The Fear and Greed Index

The **Fear and Greed Index**, popularized by CNNMoney, is a composite measure of several factors that reflect investor sentiment, such as stock price momentum, volatility, and demand for safe-haven assets like gold.

- **How to Use It:** A high level of greed often signals overbought conditions, while excessive fear can indicate oversold conditions. By watching the Fear and Greed Index, traders can assess whether the market is in an extreme sentiment zone.

Leveraging Market Sentiment in Futures Trading

Understanding sentiment allows you to time your entries and exits more effectively. Here are some ways to leverage sentiment analysis in your trading:

1. Identifying Trend Reversals

Sentiment can help you spot when a prevailing trend is likely to reverse. For example, if the market has been trending upward for an extended period and sentiment becomes excessively bullish, it could signal a top. On the other hand, if the market has been falling and sentiment becomes excessively bearish, it could indicate a buying opportunity.

2. Spotting Breakouts and Breakdowns

When sentiment shifts suddenly, it can lead to dramatic price movements, such as breakouts or breakdowns. By watching for shifts in sentiment, you can position yourself ahead of significant price moves. If sentiment turns more optimistic, it could be the catalyst for a breakout, while a shift toward pessimism could trigger a breakdown.

3. Using Sentiment for Risk Management

Market sentiment can also help with risk management. For example, if sentiment is highly optimistic but there are underlying signs of weakness, you might want to reduce your position size or tighten your stop-loss levels. Conversely, if sentiment is overly pessimistic but you spot signs of strength, you could look for opportunities to add to your positions.

Summary

Understanding and leveraging market sentiment gives traders a unique advantage. By combining sentiment analysis with technical and fundamental factors, you can develop a more comprehensive approach to trading. Market sentiment is a powerful tool for predicting market movements, spotting reversals, and managing risk, making it an essential part of any successful futures trader's toolkit.

Key Takeaways

✔ Market sentiment reflects the collective mood of market participants and plays a major role in driving price movements.

✔ Tools like the COT Report, volatility indicators, social media analysis, and market breadth indicators can help gauge sentiment.

✔ Identifying sentiment extremes can signal potential trend reversals and present profitable trading opportunities.

✔ Leveraging sentiment can improve trade timing, enhance risk management, and help spot breakouts and breakdowns.

Chapter 22

Futures Trading Algorithms and Automation – The Future of Trading

Introduction

As technology continues to evolve, automation and algorithmic trading are becoming integral parts of modern futures trading. While traditional manual trading methods have their place, the use of algorithms and automation tools has revolutionized the way traders analyze markets, place orders, and execute strategies. This chapter explores the role of algorithms and automation in futures trading, how they work, and how you can harness them to take your trading to the next level.

What Are Trading Algorithms?

A trading algorithm is a set of rules and instructions coded into a program that automatically executes trades based on predefined criteria. These criteria can include a variety of factors such as price levels, technical indicators, market sentiment, or economic data releases. Algorithms are designed to remove human emotion from the decision-making process, enabling faster and more efficient execution of trades.

Types of Trading Algorithms:

- **Trend-Following Algorithms:** These algorithms are designed to identify and capitalize on established market trends. They buy during uptrends and sell during downtrends, executing trades when specific technical indicators confirm the direction.

- **Mean Reversion Algorithms:** These strategies look for markets that have deviated from their average price levels and aim to profit from a return to the mean. These algorithms tend to focus on oversold or overbought conditions.

- **Arbitrage Algorithms:** Arbitrage strategies exploit price differences between related markets. These algorithms quickly identify price discrepancies and execute trades to take advantage of them, often within fractions of a second.

- **High-Frequency Trading (HFT):** This type of algorithmic trading involves executing a large number of orders at extremely high speeds. HFT strategies are typically used by institutional traders to capitalize on very small price movements.

How Algorithmic Trading Works in Futures Markets

Algorithmic trading relies on advanced technology and programming to execute trades efficiently. Here's an overview of how it works in futures markets:

1. **Data Gathering and Analysis:** Trading algorithms begin by gathering and analyzing large volumes of market data. This data can come from various sources such as price movements, order book information, economic indicators, and even news sentiment analysis. The algorithm processes this data to identify potential trading opportunities.

2. **Predefined Trading Strategy:** The algorithm follows a specific set of rules based on the trader's strategy. These rules can be based on technical indicators, chart patterns, or other market signals. For example, an algorithm might be programmed to buy when a moving average crosses above a certain level or when the Relative Strength Index (RSI) hits an oversold condition.

3. **Order Execution:** Once the algorithm identifies a trading signal, it automatically places an order without the need for manual intervention. This process significantly reduces the time it takes to execute trades, which is crucial in fast-moving markets like futures.

4. **Risk Management and Stop Losses:** Automated trading systems can also include built-in risk management features such as stop-loss orders, position sizing, and portfolio diversification. These features ensure that the trading algorithm can minimize losses and protect the trader's capital even when the market moves unfavorably.

Benefits of Algorithmic Trading

Algorithmic trading offers several advantages over traditional manual trading methods, making it an attractive option for many futures traders. Here are some key benefits:

1. Speed and Efficiency:

Algorithms can process vast amounts of market data and execute trades much faster than a human trader. In the high-speed world of futures trading, speed is crucial, and automation allows traders to act on opportunities almost instantaneously.

2. Elimination of Emotion:

One of the biggest challenges in trading is managing emotions. Fear, greed, and impatience can cloud judgment and lead to poor decision-making. Algorithmic trading eliminates the emotional aspect of trading, as trades are executed strictly based on the predefined strategy.

3. Backtesting Capabilities:

With algorithms, you can backtest strategies using historical data to see how they would have performed in different market conditions. This allows traders to refine their strategies before using real capital and helps identify any flaws in the approach.

4. Scalability:

Automated systems can handle a large number of trades simultaneously, allowing traders to scale their strategies across multiple futures contracts and markets. This is especially useful for high-frequency or arbitrage strategies that rely on executing many trades in a short period.

5. Consistency and Discipline:

Once an algorithm is programmed, it will execute trades consistently according to the rules set out in the strategy. This ensures that the trader sticks to their trading plan and avoids impulsive decisions based on short-term market fluctuations.

Creating Your Own Futures Trading Algorithm

Developing an algorithm for futures trading may seem like a daunting task, but with the right approach, it's entirely achievable. Here are the key steps involved:

1. Define Your Strategy:

Before you begin coding an algorithm, you need to define your trading strategy. This includes determining what indicators or patterns your algorithm will use to enter and exit trades. For example, you might design an algorithm based on moving averages, momentum indicators, or breakout strategies.

2. Choose the Right Platform:

Several platforms are available for building and testing trading algorithms, such as **MetaTrader 4/5**, **NinjaTrader**, **TradeStation**, and **QuantConnect**. These platforms allow you to code your algorithm, backtest it using historical data, and implement it in real-time markets.

3. Learn the Programming Language:

Most trading platforms require some knowledge of programming to develop an algorithm. Common languages used in algorithmic trading include **Python**, **C++**, and **JavaScript**. Python, in particular, is widely used for its simplicity and flexibility.

4. Backtest and Optimize:

Once your algorithm is ready, backtest it using historical market data. This will allow you to assess its performance and identify any weaknesses. Make sure to optimize the parameters of the algorithm to improve its risk-adjusted returns.

5. Paper Trade:

Before risking real capital, it's essential to test your algorithm in a simulated environment. Most trading platforms offer a "paper trading" feature where you can run your algorithm without actually executing live trades.

6. Go Live:

Once you've thoroughly tested and optimized your algorithm, you can deploy it to live markets. However, it's important to monitor its performance regularly to ensure that it is functioning as expected and making profitable trades.

Automated Trading vs. Manual Trading

While algorithmic trading offers several advantages, it is not without its challenges. One of the key considerations is the level of control you are willing to relinquish. In manual trading, you can adjust your strategy in real-time based on market conditions, while automated trading relies strictly on the predefined algorithm.

However, for traders who want to remove emotional bias, improve efficiency, and scale their strategies, automation provides a significant advantage. It's essential to understand the risks of algorithmic trading, such as technical failures, data inaccuracies, or slippage, and have a robust risk management system in place.

Summary

Algorithmic trading is reshaping the landscape of modern futures trading by enabling traders to execute strategies with speed, consistency, and discipline. By removing emotion and leveraging data-driven decision-making, algorithms can process complex market information and act on opportunities far faster than any human. From trend-following and mean reversion to high-frequency and arbitrage strategies, algorithmic systems provide an edge across a variety of market conditions. Building your own automated system involves selecting a platform, learning to code or using no-code tools, backtesting thoroughly, and managing risk proactively. While automation does not eliminate all risk, it empowers traders to scale operations, refine strategies, and navigate the fast-paced futures markets with confidence and control.

Key Takeaways

✔ Algorithmic trading uses predefined rules to execute trades automatically, based on market data, technical indicators, and trading strategies.

✔ Benefits of algorithmic trading include speed, consistency, emotion-free decision-making, backtesting, and scalability.

✔ Developing your own futures trading algorithm involves defining your strategy, choosing a platform, learning programming, backtesting, and paper trading

✔ Automated trading systems can improve trading efficiency, but they also come with risks such as technical failures and market volatility.

Chapter 23

Market Liquidity and Its Impact on Futures Trading

Introduction

Market liquidity is one of the most critical, yet often overlooked, factors in futures trading. A market's liquidity determines how easily you can enter and exit trades without causing significant price movement. Understanding liquidity can make a huge difference in your overall trading performance, as it impacts the spread, slippage, and the ability to execute trades at favorable prices. In this chapter, we'll explore how liquidity affects the futures market and how you can leverage this knowledge to trade smarter and more effectively.

What is Market Liquidity?

Market liquidity refers to the ability to buy or sell an asset without causing a drastic change in its price. The more liquid a market is, the easier it is to execute large trades without significantly moving the price. A market is considered highly liquid when there are a large number of buy and sell orders available at different price levels.

In futures markets, liquidity is particularly important because of the leverage involved. Futures contracts allow traders to control a large position with a relatively small margin, meaning that low liquidity can cause significant price swings, leading to greater risk. Conversely, high liquidity provides a smoother trading experience with less price slippage and more predictable order execution.

The Role of Liquidity in Futures Trading

Liquidity plays a significant role in multiple aspects of futures trading. Let's break down how liquidity affects your ability to trade and how to assess it in different market conditions:

1. Order Execution Speed:

In highly liquid markets, orders are executed almost instantly because there are many buyers and sellers. This is important for short-term traders who rely on fast execution for scalping or intraday trades. Conversely, in illiquid markets, there may be delays in execution, leading to missed opportunities or unfavorable fills.

2. Bid-Ask Spread:

The bid-ask spread represents the difference between the highest price a buyer is willing to pay (bid) and the lowest price a seller is willing to accept (ask). In liquid markets, the spread is typically smaller because of the large number of market participants. This can reduce trading costs since you pay less to enter or exit a position. In contrast, illiquid markets tend to have larger spreads, which can eat into your profits.

3. Slippage:

Slippage occurs when an order is filled at a different price than expected, often due to low liquidity. For example, if you place an order to buy a futures contract at $100, but the order is filled at $101, that's slippage. Slippage can be particularly problematic during volatile periods, where the price moves rapidly. In highly liquid markets, slippage is generally minimal, and your orders are more likely to fill at or near the expected price.

4. Price Volatility and Risk Management:

Low liquidity tends to exacerbate price volatility. When fewer participants are trading a particular contract, large trades can move the market significantly, leading to sharp price fluctuations. For traders, this means higher risk. On the other hand, a more liquid market tends to have smoother price movements, reducing the risk of sudden price reversals and improving the predictability of price action.

How to Assess Liquidity in the Futures Market

There are several ways to assess liquidity in futures markets. Here's how you can evaluate liquidity for the contracts you plan to trade:

1. Volume:

Trading volume is one of the most straightforward indicators of liquidity. Higher trading volumes generally indicate a higher level of liquidity. Look at the average daily volume for the futures contracts you're considering. Higher volume means there are more market participants, making it easier to enter or exit trades. Conversely, low volume indicates lower liquidity, which could result in wider bid-ask spreads and more slippage.

2. Open Interest:

Open interest refers to the total number of outstanding contracts that haven't been settled. It can provide insight into the strength of a market. High open interest generally indicates that there are more participants and, thus, higher liquidity. A sudden drop in open interest may signal a lack of participation and decreased liquidity.

3. Order Book Depth:

The depth of the order book reflects how many orders exist at various price levels. A deep order book with many buy and sell orders at various price points signals good liquidity. Conversely, a shallow order book with few orders can result in more price fluctuations when executing large trades.

4. Market Conditions:

Liquidity can fluctuate based on market conditions. For example, during times of market uncertainty, such as economic crises or major geopolitical events, liquidity tends to dry up, and spreads can widen. During stable market conditions, liquidity is typically more abundant.

Trading Strategies for High and Low Liquidity Markets

Your approach to trading can change depending on the liquidity of the market you're dealing with. Here's how to adjust your strategy in both high and low liquidity conditions:

1. High Liquidity Markets:

In liquid markets, you can afford to use more aggressive strategies like scalping or intraday trading. These strategies rely on quick, small price moves, so executing orders rapidly and efficiently is crucial. Because slippage is minimal, these strategies tend to be more reliable and profitable in highly liquid markets.

2. Low Liquidity Markets:

In illiquid markets, you'll need to be more cautious with your trades. Large trades can impact the market price significantly, so it's important to avoid slippage and manage risk more conservatively. Strategies like swing trading or trend following may be more appropriate in these environments since they rely on longer-term price movements. Additionally, using limit orders instead of market orders can help you control your entry price and minimize slippage.

Managing Risk in Low Liquidity Markets

In low liquidity environments, the risk of significant price swings increases. To mitigate these risks, consider the following tips:

- **Use Limit Orders:** Always place limit orders to control your entry and exit points. This ensures that you're not subject to slippage when trying to fill your position.

- **Adjust Position Sizing:** Reduce the size of your trades to limit exposure, especially when liquidity is thin. This allows you to trade more safely without risking too much capital in one trade.

- **Monitor Market Depth:** Keep a close eye on the order book and bid-ask spread to identify potential liquidity shortages before entering trades.

- **Use Tight Stop-Losses:** In volatile, low-liquidity markets, you need to use tighter stop-losses to limit your losses if the market moves unexpectedly.

Summary

In this chapter, we explored the importance of market liquidity and how it affects futures trading. Market liquidity refers to the ability of a market to facilitate the buying and selling of assets without causing significant price movements. High liquidity generally results in smaller spreads and faster execution, while low liquidity can lead to wider spreads and higher slippage, making it more difficult to execute trades at the desired price.

We also discussed how to assess market liquidity by analyzing factors like volume, open interest, and order book depth. Traders need to understand how liquidity varies across different markets and adapt their strategies accordingly. In highly liquid markets, traders can use aggressive strategies with tighter risk management, while in illiquid markets, they may need to employ more conservative methods and reduce their position size to avoid significant slippage.

Key Takeaways

✔ **Market liquidity** is essential for smooth trade execution, influencing speed, slippage, and volatility.

✔ **High liquidity** markets offer smaller bid-ask spreads, faster executions, and less slippage, making them ideal for intraday trading strategies.

✔ **Low liquidity** markets result in larger spreads and more price fluctuations, requiring a more cautious approach with limited trade size and stricter risk management.

✔ Use **volume**, **open interest**, and **order book depth** to assess market liquidity and plan your trades effectively.

✔ Adjust your strategy in illiquid markets by using **limit orders**, reducing **position size**, and **tightening stop-losses** to mitigate risk.

Chapter 24

Understanding and Trading Different Types of Futures Contracts

Introduction

In futures trading, one of the most important decisions you'll make is selecting the right type of futures contract to trade. Each type of contract has its unique characteristics and uses, so it's crucial to understand these differences in order to align your strategy with the right product. This chapter explores the most common types of futures contracts—commodity, financial, currency, and interest rate futures—and offers insights on how to trade them effectively.

Commodity Futures Contracts

Commodity futures are contracts that allow traders to buy or sell a specific quantity of a physical commodity at a future date for an agreed-upon price. These are some of the most widely traded futures contracts, particularly in markets like agriculture, energy, and precious metals.

- **Agricultural Commodities**: These contracts involve products like wheat, corn, soybeans, and livestock. They are popular among traders looking to profit from price fluctuations in the agricultural sector, often influenced by factors such as weather, crop yields, and geopolitical

events.
Example: Corn futures allow traders to speculate on the price of corn. If they expect prices to rise, they can go long, while shorting the contract would be an option if they expect prices to fall.

- **Energy Commodities**: This includes oil (crude and refined), natural gas, and other energy-related products. The energy sector is highly volatile, driven by global supply and demand, geopolitical factors, and economic conditions.
  Example: Crude oil futures are one of the most liquid markets. Traders use them to profit from oil price swings, whether driven by OPEC announcements or shifts in global production.

- **Precious Metals**: Gold, silver, platinum, and other precious metals are commonly traded in futures markets. These commodities act as safe havens during times of economic uncertainty, making them popular among traders looking for diversification.
  Example: Gold futures are often traded when economic uncertainty arises. Investors use them to hedge against inflation and market instability.

Financial Futures Contracts

Financial futures contracts allow traders to speculate on the future value of a financial asset. These contracts can involve stock indices, treasury bonds, and other instruments tied to the financial markets.

- **Stock Index Futures**: These contracts represent a basket of stocks that track a specific stock index, such as the S&P 500, NASDAQ-100, or Dow Jones Industrial Average. They provide traders with a way to gain exposure to the broader market without having to buy individual stocks.
  Example: S&P 500 futures offer exposure to the overall performance of the U.S. stock market. Traders use these contracts to hedge risk or speculate on market movements.

- **Treasury Futures**: Treasury futures allow traders to speculate on U.S. government debt. These contracts are based on U.S. Treasury securities like bonds, notes, and bills. They are often used by institutional investors and central banks to hedge interest rate risk.
  Example: 10-year Treasury futures are commonly traded by traders who expect interest rate changes, providing opportunities to profit from shifting yields.

Currency Futures Contracts

Currency futures are contracts to buy or sell a currency at a future date for a set price. They allow traders to profit from fluctuations in the value of currencies. Currency futures are particularly useful for those looking to hedge against foreign exchange risks or speculate on global economic conditions.

- **Popular Currency Pairs**: Some of the most commonly traded currency futures involve the U.S. Dollar, such as EUR/USD (Euro/US Dollar), GBP/USD (British Pound/US Dollar), and JPY/USD (Japanese Yen/US Dollar). **Example**: EUR/USD futures enable traders to speculate on the exchange rate between the Euro and U.S. Dollar. If a trader believes the Euro will strengthen, they would go long, whereas shorting would profit from the Euro weakening.

- **Global Implications**: Currency futures can be influenced by geopolitical events, trade policies, and central bank decisions, offering opportunities to trade based on global economic news and developments.

Interest Rate Futures Contracts

Interest rate futures are contracts based on the future direction of interest rates. These contracts can be used by traders to speculate on interest rate changes, hedge against interest rate risk, or profit from changes in bond yields.

- **Fed Funds Futures**: These futures are based on the U.S. Federal Reserve's short-term interest rates. Traders use them to speculate on the direction of U.S. monetary policy, with particular interest in upcoming Federal Open Market Committee (FOMC) meetings and potential rate changes.
  Example: Fed Funds futures can signal traders' expectations about future rate hikes or cuts, providing insight into economic conditions and central bank actions.

- **Eurodollar Futures**: These contracts are tied to the U.S. dollar interest rate on deposits held outside the United States. They are highly liquid and frequently used by institutional traders.
  Example: Eurodollar futures are often used by institutional investors and hedge funds to speculate on interest rate movements and global liquidity.

Which Futures Contract Should You Trade?

The type of futures contract you trade depends on several factors, including your trading goals, risk tolerance, and market analysis. Here are some tips to help you decide:

- **Commodity Futures**: If you're interested in global supply and demand dynamics, or if you have an interest in sectors like agriculture or energy, commodity futures might be a good fit. They tend to be more volatile and reactive to external events.

- **Financial Futures**: For those looking to trade based on broader economic and financial market trends, financial futures offer access to markets like stock indices and Treasury bonds. These are popular among traders looking for less volatility compared to commodities.

- **Currency Futures**: Currency futures are ideal for traders interested in global economics and central bank policy. They offer high liquidity and the potential for significant price movements due to geopolitical events.

- **Interest Rate Futures**: If you have an understanding of economic cycles and monetary policy, interest rate futures can provide a solid opportunity for speculation and hedging.

Summary

Choosing the right futures contract is crucial to your success in futures trading. Whether you focus on commodities, financial products, currencies, or interest rates, understanding the specific characteristics of each contract allows you to tailor your strategy and manage your risk effectively. By selecting the futures contract that aligns with your trading goals, you can enhance your ability to profit from the market while controlling your risk exposure.

Key Takeaways

✔ Commodity futures include agricultural, energy, and precious metal contracts.

✔ Financial futures include stock index and treasury contracts, suitable for speculating on broader market trends.

✔ Currency futures focus on the value of global currencies, influenced by economic policies and events.

✔ Interest rate futures are used for speculation and hedging based on interest rate movements.

✔ Choosing the right type of futures contract depends on your goals and risk tolerance.

Chapter 25

Seasonal Trends and Market Cycles – How to Leverage Time-of-Year Patterns for Trading Futures

Introduction

In futures trading, many traders focus on technical indicators and chart patterns to predict price movements. However, there's another often-overlooked aspect that can significantly impact price behavior: seasonal trends. These trends are driven by predictable factors like weather, fiscal calendars, and even geopolitical events that occur at specific times throughout the year. By understanding these cycles, traders can position themselves to take advantage of market behaviors that recur with regularity.

In this chapter, we'll dive into how seasonal trends and market cycles influence futures prices, helping you spot patterns that occur throughout the year. These insights can give you an edge in understanding what might happen in the future, based on historical data.

What Are Seasonal Trends?

Seasonal trends are predictable price movements that occur at specific times during the year due to recurring external factors. These could be linked to agricultural cycles, energy consumption patterns, weather-related events, and even political or fiscal cycles that influence market sentiment.

For example, oil prices typically rise in the summer months due to increased demand for gasoline as travel and consumption peak during vacations. Similarly, agricultural commodities like wheat or corn experience seasonal price shifts based on planting and harvest schedules.

Identifying Key Seasonal Trends in Futures Markets

To capitalize on seasonal trends, it's essential to identify the commodities or assets that exhibit consistent behavior during certain periods. Here's a look at some of the most common seasonal trends for futures traders:

1. **Energy Futures (Crude Oil, Natural Gas)**
   - **Winter and Summer Weather Patterns:** Demand for natural gas spikes in the winter due to heating needs, while oil prices often rise during the summer months when driving demand for gasoline

increases.

- **Geopolitical Factors:** Certain months, like the spring or fall, often coincide with OPEC meetings, where oil production levels are discussed, creating volatility in oil prices.

2. **Agricultural Commodities (Wheat, Corn, Soybeans, Coffee)**

- **Planting and Harvest Seasons:** Agricultural commodities like corn and soybeans experience seasonal fluctuations based on planting and harvest periods. Prices can rise just before harvest when there's uncertainty about crop yields, and fall after harvest as supply increases.

- **Weather Events:** Adverse weather, such as droughts or floods, can cause crop failures and lead to price spikes in agricultural commodities, especially during the growing season.

3. **Precious Metals (Gold, Silver)**

   - **Holiday Season Demand:** Gold and silver often see increased demand in the months leading up to the holiday season as consumers purchase jewelry and other products for gifts. Additionally, gold can act as a hedge during times of economic uncertainty, which tends to peak at specific points in the year.

   - **Indian Wedding Season:** Gold prices often rise during the Indian wedding season, typically between October and December, as demand for jewelry surges.

4. **Stock Indices (S&P 500, Dow Jones)**

   - **End-of-Year Rally:** The stock market has historically seen a "Santa Claus Rally" in the last weeks of December, where stocks tend to rise due to holiday optimism and institutional buying. Similarly, the first few months of the year are often marked by a continuation of this trend.

- **Earnings Season:** Corporate earnings reports that come out in the first quarter can have a significant impact on stock prices, causing temporary volatility in indices like the S&P 500.

Leveraging Seasonal Trends in Your Futures Trading Strategy

Understanding when to anticipate seasonal movements can give traders a significant advantage. Here's how to integrate these trends into your futures trading strategy:

1. **Use Historical Data:** Review historical data for the asset you're trading to spot recurring patterns during specific times of the year. You can analyze price movements for several years to determine the consistency of these trends.

2. **Combine Seasonal Trends with Technical Analysis:** Once you've identified a potential seasonal trend, use technical indicators (e.g., moving averages, Bollinger Bands, or RSI) to confirm your entry or exit signals. For example, if you spot a seasonal price increase in oil during the summer months, look for technical indicators

that suggest a bullish market.

3. **Plan Your Risk Management:** While seasonal trends can be reliable, they aren't guaranteed. Always employ risk management strategies like stop-loss orders and position sizing to protect yourself from unforeseen market movements.

4. **Adapt to Changing Conditions:** Seasonal trends are not static. Always adapt your strategy if you notice changes in economic conditions, market sentiment, or external factors that could impact the trends you're trading. For instance, extreme weather events like hurricanes can have a large impact on commodity prices and may disrupt seasonal trends.

The Role of Economic Cycles in Futures Trading

In addition to specific seasonal trends, broader economic cycles can play a significant role in futures markets. Understanding the phases of the economic cycle—expansion, peak, recession, and recovery—can help you predict when different assets are likely to perform well.

- **Expansion and Recovery:** In the early stages of an economic recovery, commodities like oil and metals may see an uptick in demand as industrial activity increases. Stock indices may also benefit from increased corporate earnings.

- **Recession:** During periods of economic slowdown, traders may turn to safe-haven assets like gold or US Treasury bonds. Agricultural commodities can also experience volatility, as lower consumer spending and less disposable income can affect demand.

Understanding the stage of the economic cycle allows you to take a longer-term view of potential market movements.

Practical Example: Trading Wheat Futures During the Growing Season

Let's apply what we've learned in a practical example. Wheat is an agricultural commodity that experiences seasonal fluctuations tied to planting and harvest times. In the spring, as planting season approaches, wheat prices can rise due to uncertainty over weather conditions, particularly the risk of droughts or floods that could impact yield.

A trader who understands this seasonal trend might look to enter a long position in wheat futures around late winter, when prices begin to show signs of upward momentum, and exit after harvest when supply increases and prices typically fall. This strategy allows the trader to capitalize on the seasonal cycle while using technical analysis tools to fine-tune their entry and exit points.

Summary

Incorporating seasonal trends into your futures trading strategy can offer a valuable edge. By understanding the cyclical nature of various commodities, indices, and even broader economic patterns, you can anticipate price movements and plan your trades accordingly.

However, while these trends are historically reliable, they should always be used in conjunction with technical analysis and solid risk management practices. With the right tools and strategies, you can leverage seasonal trends and market cycles to enhance your trading success and boost profitability.

Key Takeaways

✔ Seasonal trends are recurring patterns in price behavior driven by factors like weather, fiscal calendars, and geopolitical events.

✔ Crude oil, natural gas, agricultural commodities, metals, and stock indices all exhibit seasonal tendencies that can be anticipated.

✔ Combine seasonal analysis with technical indicators for higher-probability trade setups.

✔ Use historical data to identify consistent seasonal patterns in the assets you trade.

✔ Be aware of the broader economic cycle, as expansion and recession phases impact futures markets differently.

✔ Always use proper risk management when trading seasonal patterns—no trend is guaranteed every year.

Chapter 26

Futures Trading Tax Essentials – Understanding Your Obligations and Advantages

Introduction

While most traders focus on strategy and execution, few spend enough time understanding the tax implications of their futures trading. Knowing how your trades are taxed—and how to legally minimize your tax liability—is a vital part of being a successful, long-term trader. This chapter breaks down the key tax rules, reporting requirements, and advantages available to U.S.-based futures traders under IRS Section 1256.

What Makes Futures Taxation Unique?

Unlike stocks or options, U.S. futures contracts are taxed under the favorable **Section 1256 tax treatment**, which offers two significant advantages:

- **60/40 Tax Split**: Profits from Section 1256 contracts are taxed as **60% long-term capital gains** and **40% short-term capital gains**—regardless of how long the trade was held.

- **Mark-to-Market Accounting**: At year-end, your futures positions are treated as if they were sold at fair market value, meaning both realized and unrealized gains/losses are reported annually.

This setup often leads to **lower overall tax rates** for active traders compared to stock traders.

What Instruments Fall Under Section 1256?

Section 1256 applies to:

- **Regulated futures contracts** (e.g., oil, gold, index futures)
- **Index options** (e.g., SPX options)
- **Foreign currency contracts** traded on regulated exchanges

However, it **does not apply to**:

- Forex spot trading
- Single stock futures (depending on exchange)

- Options on individual stocks

Make sure your broker provides clarity on which instruments fall under Section 1256.

Understanding Form 6781

If you trade Section 1256 contracts, you'll use **IRS Form 6781** to report your gains and losses.

Breakdown of Form 6781:

- **Part I**: Lists your net gains/losses from Section 1256 contracts.
- **Line 1**: Shows your year-end mark-to-market amount.
- **Line 9**: Carries over the 60/40 split to your tax return (Schedule D).

You don't need to itemize every individual trade—just the net figure, which simplifies filing.

Benefits of the 60/40 Tax Split

Let's say you made $100,000 in futures profits:

- $60,000 is taxed at the **long-term capital gains rate** (often 15%)

- $40,000 is taxed at the **short-term capital gains rate** (your regular income tax rate)

This can dramatically reduce your tax bill compared to stock trading, where short-term trades are 100% taxed at your income rate.

What About Trading Losses?

Losses from Section 1256 contracts **can offset gains**, and if your losses exceed your gains for the year, you can carry the loss forward to offset future gains.

Example:

- You lose $10,000 this year on futures.
- You make $30,000 next year.
- You can reduce next year's taxable gain to $20,000.

Should You Form an LLC or S-Corp?

For many retail futures traders, trading as an individual is sufficient. However, forming an entity like an **LLC or S-Corp** may be useful for:

- **Business expense deductions**
- **Health insurance write-offs**
- **Retirement account contributions**

It's recommended to consult a CPA familiar with trader taxation before setting up an entity.

Record Keeping & Reporting Best Practices

Even though you only report net gains or losses on Form 6781, you should still keep detailed records:

- Entry and exit prices
- Contract specifications
- Trade duration
- Notes on trade rationale
- Broker statements

Good records also help if you're ever audited.

Hiring a Tax Professional

Futures tax law can get complex quickly. Consider working with a **tax advisor who specializes in active trading**. A qualified CPA can help you:

- Maximize legal deductions
- Structure your trading activities
- File your tax returns accurately

Summary

Understanding how futures are taxed is essential for keeping more of your profits and avoiding surprises at tax time. Unlike stocks, most futures contracts fall under the IRS's Section 1256, which offers favorable tax treatment through a 60/40 split between long-term and short-term capital gains—regardless of holding period. This can significantly lower your overall tax bill. By keeping accurate records, working with a tax professional, and knowing how mark-to-market rules apply, you can file with confidence and plan your trading year more effectively.

Key Takeaways

✔ Most futures contracts are taxed under IRS Section 1256, using a 60% long-term / 40% short-term capital gains split.

✔ Section 1256 gains and losses are reported on IRS Form 6781.

✔ Mark-to-market rules mean your open futures positions are treated as sold on the last trading day of the year.

✔ Accurate trade logs and professional guidance are key to proper reporting and maximizing tax efficiency.

✔ State tax laws may vary, so check local requirements or consult a CPA familiar with trading.

Chapter 27

Leveraging Volume Analysis – Decoding Market Participation for Better Trades

Introduction

In futures trading, price is only part of the story. Volume—the total number of contracts traded during a given time period—offers critical insights into market strength, conviction, and participation. When used effectively, volume analysis can help you filter out false breakouts, confirm trends, and time entries with more confidence. In this chapter, we'll explore how to leverage volume to enhance your strategy and make smarter, data-driven trading decisions.

Understanding Volume in Futures Trading

Volume represents the level of activity in a futures contract. Higher volume typically indicates stronger interest or conviction in a price move, while low volume may signal weakness or consolidation.

Key Concepts:

- **Volume Spikes:** Sudden increases in volume can signal institutional activity or news-driven moves.

- **Volume Clusters:** Sustained high-volume zones may become areas of support/resistance.
- **Volume Gaps:** Areas with very low historical volume can lead to fast price movement when revisited.

Why Volume Matters

Volume helps traders distinguish between real breakouts and fakeouts. A breakout backed by strong volume is more likely to sustain than one with weak participation.

- **Confirming Breakouts:** Use volume to validate price breaking through key levels.
- **Identifying Exhaustion:** A rising market with declining volume may suggest weakening momentum.
- **Locating Liquidity Zones:** High-volume areas often become "battlegrounds" where traders previously entered or exited positions.

Powerful Volume-Based Indicators

You can gain deeper insight into market activity by using volume-based tools. Here are a few of the most powerful:

1. Volume Profile

Displays traded volume at each price level rather than over time. Highlights high-volume nodes (HVNs) and low-volume nodes (LVNs).

- **Use it to:** Identify value areas, support/resistance, and breakout levels.

2. On-Balance Volume (OBV)

Cumulative volume indicator that rises when volume is up on bullish days and falls when it's down on bearish days.

- **Use it to:** Spot divergence between price and volume to anticipate reversals.

3. Accumulation/Distribution Line

Uses both price and volume to assess whether a stock or contract is being accumulated or distributed.

- **Use it to:** Track underlying buying or selling pressure.

4. Volume Weighted Average Price (VWAP)

A moving average weighted by volume. Often used by institutions to evaluate fair value throughout the trading day.

- **Use it to:** Guide intraday trend bias and as dynamic support/resistance.

5. Money Flow Index (MFI)

Combines price and volume in a momentum oscillator, similar to RSI but volume-weighted.

- **Use it to:** Identify overbought/oversold conditions with more context than RSI alone.

Advanced Volume Tactics

If you want to take your volume game to the next level, here are a few pro-level tips:

- **Pair with Candlestick Patterns:** Volume can confirm the validity of reversal patterns like hammers or engulfing candles.

- **Look for Volume Dry-Ups Before Moves:** Tight consolidation with declining volume often precedes explosive breakouts.

- **Compare Volume Across Timeframes:** Use a top-down approach to see if volume aligns on the higher timeframes with what you see intraday.

Summary

Volume is a powerful yet underutilized tool in futures trading. While price shows you *what* is happening, volume reveals *how strongly* it's happening. Integrating volume analysis into your strategy helps you avoid traps, spot smart money moves, and execute with greater confidence.

Key Takeaways

✔ Volume shows the intensity behind price moves and helps confirm breakout or reversal strength.

✔ Volume Profile and VWAP are powerful tools for locating key levels and understanding intraday value.

✔ Volume indicators like OBV and Accumulation/Distribution reveal hidden buying and selling pressure.

✔ Use volume dry-ups, spikes, and clusters to anticipate future price behavior.

✔ Combine volume analysis with candlesticks and technical indicators for a more complete trading edge.

Chapter 28

Futures Trading and Global Markets – Adapting to International Influence

Introduction

Futures markets may be U.S.-based, but their heartbeat is global. International economies, foreign currencies, overseas stock exchanges, and geopolitical shifts all play a role in how futures move—especially contracts tied to commodities and global indices. Whether it's a surge in the Nikkei 225 during the Asian session or an ECB policy decision during European hours, futures traders must understand the global landscape to make informed decisions.

Let's break down how to navigate the global factors that directly impact your futures trades and how to turn that knowledge into a strategic edge.

Global Trading Sessions and Their Influence

Asian, European, and U.S. Market Hours

Markets move in cycles across global time zones. Understanding when major exchanges are active helps traders anticipate when volume and volatility might increase.

- **Asian Session (Tokyo, Shanghai, etc.)**
    - Roughly 7:00 PM – 3:00 AM EST.
    - Gold (GC) and crude oil (CL) can become active during this session due to Asian demand.
    - Watch for movements in the Nikkei 225, Chinese manufacturing data, and Australian economic releases.
- **European Session (London, Frankfurt)**
    - Roughly 3:00 AM – 11:30 AM EST.
    - Often overlaps with the latter part of the Asian session and the early U.S. session.
    - The Euro, DAX, and UK news can significantly move indexes like the ES or NQ.

- **U.S. Session**
    - 9:30 AM – 4:00 PM EST (cash market), with futures trading 23 hours/day.
    - U.S. economic releases often hit at 8:30 AM EST, so premarket volatility is common.

Overlapping Hours = High Impact

When sessions overlap (e.g., London and New York), market liquidity and movement tend to spike. These are prime trading times for high-volume futures traders.

Currency and Commodity Correlations

Understanding the relationships between currencies and commodities can reveal opportunities or warn of potential risks.

Examples:

- **USD and Gold (GC):** A falling dollar often leads to higher gold prices.
- **USD and Crude Oil (CL):** Oil is priced in USD globally; a stronger dollar can suppress oil prices.
- **EUR/USD and U.S. Index Futures (ES/NQ):** A strong Euro can sometimes indicate increased investor confidence in European markets and may impact U.S. equities indirectly.

Global Economic Reports to Watch

You don't need to track every report in every country—but you *should* be aware of a few key global events that can shake the futures markets.

Important Reports:

- **ECB Press Conferences & Interest Rate Decisions**
- **Bank of Japan (BoJ) and Reserve Bank of Australia (RBA) policy statements**
- **German Manufacturing & Employment Data**
- **Chinese PMI and GDP**
- **OPEC meetings (for CL futures)**

These events often hit during overnight hours, but their effects can spill into the U.S. trading day or even shape the market tone for an entire week.

Futures and Geopolitical Risk

War, natural disasters, trade deals, and diplomatic tensions can have an immediate impact on futures.

Futures That React Quickly:

- **Crude Oil (CL):** Highly sensitive to Middle East tensions, OPEC decisions, or disruptions in shipping routes like the Suez Canal.
- **Gold (GC):** A go-to safe haven during political or economic uncertainty.
- **Index Futures (ES, NQ, YM):** React to everything from NATO summits to sudden policy shifts between global powers.

Global headlines can spike or drop markets within minutes—so staying plugged into reputable news sources or using automated news alerts is crucial.

Adapting to a Global Market Mindset

Here's how futures traders can stay ahead:

- **Use an Economic Calendar:** Track not just U.S. events but global ones too.
- **Pre-market Prep:** Check what happened in Asia and Europe before the U.S. open.
- **Watch Forex Pairs:** Currencies often respond faster to global news, giving early signals.
- **Avoid "Tunnel Vision":** Don't focus solely on U.S. data; global context builds stronger bias and trade setups.

Summary

While your trades may execute on a U.S. exchange, the forces that shape price action often originate thousands of miles away. By incorporating a global perspective, futures traders can time their trades more accurately, understand overnight price movement, and capitalize on the full 24-hour cycle. The world is interconnected—and in futures, awareness of global market behavior isn't optional, it's essential.

Key Takeaways

✔ Understand the impact of major global market sessions and overlapping hours on futures volatility.

✔ Monitor correlations between currencies and futures contracts like oil and gold.

✔ Stay aware of critical foreign economic reports and policy decisions.

✔ Use global market context to anticipate price movement and manage trades around risk events.

✔ Incorporate a world-view mindset to refine your edge in the futures markets.

Chapter 29

Final Thoughts – Your Futures Trading Journey Begins Now

You've made it to the end of *The Beginner's Blueprint to Day Trading Futures* — and that's an accomplishment worth celebrating. By now, you've built a strong foundation in futures trading, from understanding contract specs and risk management to mastering indicators, strategies, and the psychology behind every trade.

But this book isn't the finish line — it's your launchpad. Futures trading is a dynamic, fast-paced world that rewards discipline, consistency, and continued growth. No trader becomes profitable overnight, but those who persist, journal every move, refine their strategies, and never stop learning often find themselves miles ahead of the crowd.

Remember, success in trading isn't about chasing every move — it's about controlling your mindset, managing your risk, and executing your edge with precision. You've been equipped with the tools, insights, and frameworks to do exactly that.

Now it's time to take action.

Start small. Trade smart. Review relentlessly. Keep refining. And most importantly, don't give up when things get tough. Every pro trader you admire started where you are right now — unsure, hungry, and full of potential.

This is your moment. The futures market is waiting — go claim your edge.

Key Takeaways

✔ The real trading journey begins after education execution, review, and discipline are what bring results.

✔ Every chapter in this book is a stepping stone, revisit them as you level up in your trading.

✔ Stay committed to continuous improvement, because consistency beats intensity over the long run.

✔ You don't have to be perfect — you just need to be better each day.

"Every great trader was once a beginner who refused to quit — now it's your turn."

www.ingramcontent.com/pod-product-compliance
Lightning Source LLC
LaVergne TN
LVHW052248200926
848481LV00002B/311
9798349518959